DUNCAN LITTLE studied History at the University of Surrey from 1993 to 1996 before heading to Falmouth College of Arts where he qualified as a broadcast journalist in 1997. In the same year he started his career in television at ITV Westcountry, where he worked in news and current affairs. He researched, produced and directed the highly acclaimed *West Country Top Secret* television series which examined world, national and regional events during the Cold War. The six programmes won a 'Special Jury REMI Award' at the 2005 WorldFest International Film Festival. He continues to work both in news production and in the making of factual programmes.

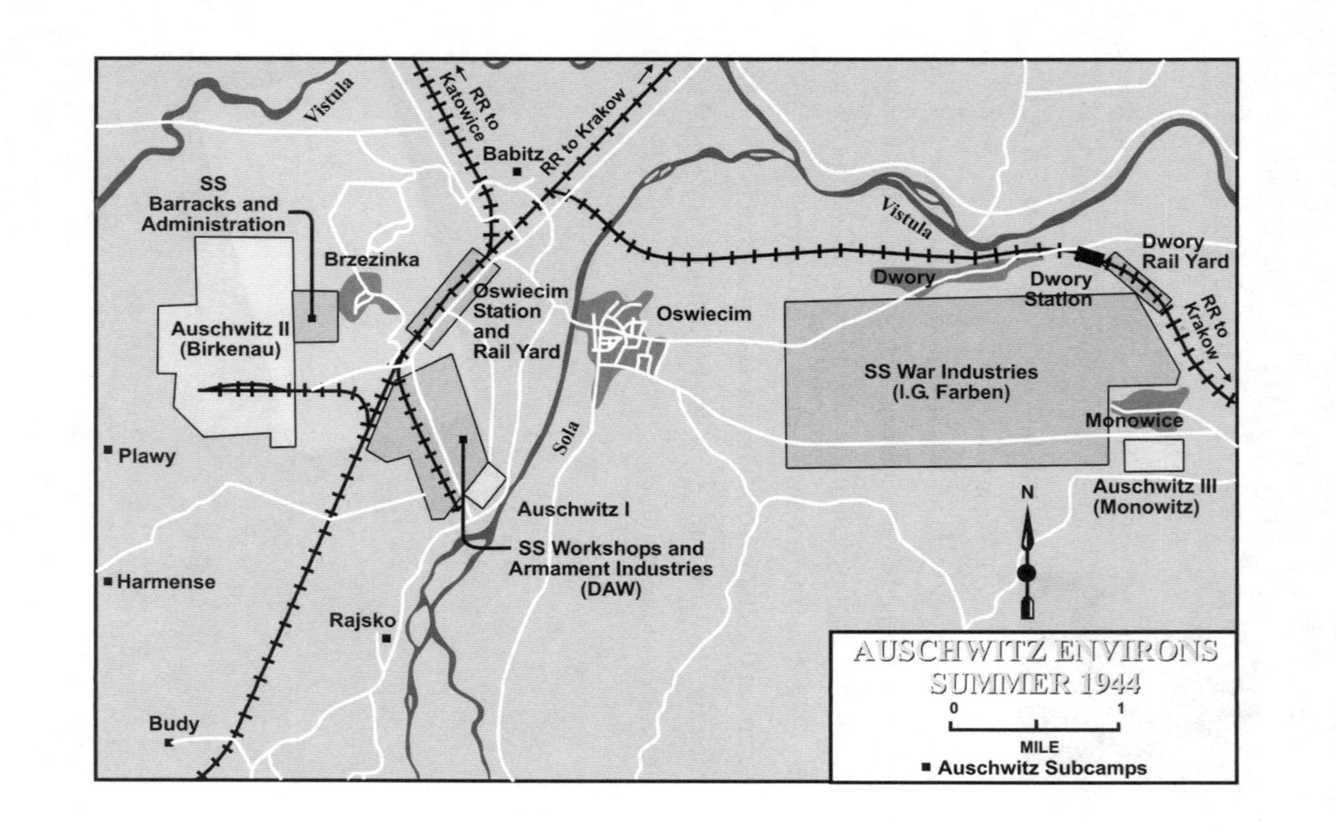
AUSCHWITZ ENVIRONS
SUMMER 1944
0
1
MILE
■ Auschwitz Subcamps
Vistula
← RR to Katowice
RR to Krakow →
Babitz
SS
Barracks and
Administration
Brzezinka
Auschwitz II
(Birkenau)
Oswiecim
Station
and
Rail Yard
Oswiecim
Sola
Auschwitz I
SS Workshops and
Armament Industries
(DAW)
Plawy
Harmense
Rajsko
Budy
Vistula
Dwory
Dwory
Station
Dwory
Rail Yard
RR to
Krakow →
SS War Industries
(I.G. Farben)
Monowice
Auschwitz III
(Monowitz)
N

Allies in Auschwitz

The Untold Story of British POWs Held Captive in the Nazis' Most Infamous Death Camp

Duncan Little

CLAIRVIEW

Clairview Books
Hillside House, The Square
Forest Row, East Sussex RH18 5ES

www.clairviewbooks.com

Published by Clairview 2009

A catalogue record for this book is available from the British Library

ISBN 978 1 905570 21 8

Cover by Andrew Morgan Design incorporating a photograph of British
POWs in E715 Auschwitz in 1944 (with Doug Bond in the front, centre)
Typeset by DP Photosetting, Neath, West Glamorgan
Printed and bound by Gutenberg Press Ltd, Malta

The paper used for this book is FSC-certified and
totally chlorine-free. FSC (the Forest Stewardship
Council) is an international network to promote
responsible management of the world's forests.

Contents

Acknowledgements vi

Introduction 1

1. Background 6

2. Cattle Trucks to Auschwitz 13

3. Recollections 18

4. The Long Walk to Freedom and Recovery 50

5. The Official Record 68

Notes 88

Acknowledgements

Firstly, thank you to Beth Rose, Phaedra, Colin and also my father for painstakingly reading through all of my work and making various helpful suggestions along the way. Mischa Loughnane kindly researched a large number of documents and papers which have proved vital for this book and I am very grateful for her help. I would also like to thank Dr Todd Gray for the coffee and encouragement which spurred me to write this book. His enthusiasm for the project led to months of research and interviews. I truly believe the final book is an important testimony to a forgotten part of our history.

I should make reference to Colin Rushton's book *Spectator in Hell*, which followed the story of a British POW who was imprisoned in Auschwitz during World War II.

Thank you to the staff at the National Archives and the Imperial War Museum. I spent a large amount of research time at both locations and ploughed my way through a colossal number of documents. Their help during this process was immensely valuable.

Finally, I am so grateful and appreciative to the men who allowed me to interview them regarding their experiences: Doug Bond, Arthur Gifford-England and Brian Bishop.

Introduction

We are all familiar with the image of Steve McQueen in *The Great Escape* and the iconic image portrayed by Hollywood concerning life as a POW in German camps. The truth, however, is very different. This book is the story of a group of men who maintained their rights as POWs but were sent to a prisoner of war camp situated on the outskirts of the Third Reich's largest death camp.

The British prisoners of E715 Auschwitz were first hand witnesses to the Nazis' brutal treatment of the Jews that culminated in the Final Solution. Very little is known of their story and their experiences were largely forgotten, or ignored, in post-war Britain.

Their POW camp was to the east of the main complex and around 400 yards from the Monowitz concentration camp. The area was known as Auschwitz III and was sited to the south of the River Vistula. A railway line (to Krakow) passed close to their camp. The British POWs were forced to work alongside concentration camp inmates in a Nazi factory, and the men witnessed daily killings around them.

The retention of their POW status afforded them certain rights – including access to Red Cross parcels. After the war, many of these men recounted how this lifeline was vital in preserving their strength. There was little they could do to help the concentration camp inmates and they could only watch as the Jews were frequently murdered in front of them. They could also smell the bodies being burnt in the crematoria and, when they were resting in their barracks, would hear Jews being shot in the nearby concentration camp.

The British prisoners underwent their own hardships as they simply were not equipped to deal with living and working in temperatures many degrees below zero. Despite the delivery of Red Cross parcels, they were provided with little food and this commodity was often scarce. A number of men within the group were beaten, one was murdered by a guard and a few were sentenced to hard labour in the nearby coal mines. There were also reports that some British men were sent into special punishment cells which were designed to cause severe cramp as they were too small to either stand up or lay down.

The surviving men's final ordeal was to march hundreds of miles, in the depths of winter, to secure their freedom in the spring of 1945.

This book charts the true story of these men: from their arrival on cattle trucks through to their departure, on foot, at the start of 1945. It contains interviews with the few surviving members of E715 Auschwitz and, in particular, it focuses on the story of one man: Brian Bishop. He was in his early twenties when he was imprisoned at the camp and what he witnessed haunted him for years afterwards.

For the majority of his life, Brian was unable to talk about what he saw. He could not bring himself to tell his wife, his family or his closest friends. He only began to recount his experiences, and finally tell his story, when research for this book started in 2006. For the first time in more than 60 years, Brian has provided an overview of what daily life was like for the prisoners of E715 Auschwitz.

The book also contains interviews with Doug Bond and Arthur Gifford-England. They were both sent to E715 Auschwitz and, like Brian, were interviewed between 2006 and 2009.

It is important to remember that people's ability to recall details and events can become distorted by the distance of time. I have, therefore, sought to cross-reference each of these men's individual testimonies with the other members of this small group. I hope this exercise has successfully ensured a clearer, more accurate picture of events. They all independently agree on the conditions and the events that are reported in this book regarding their time in Auschwitz as being accurate.

Much attention has, rightly, been placed on the exceptionally poor conditions endured by Allied soldiers abused by Japanese guards during the war. It is perhaps not surprising that the focus for wartime abuse lies in the Far East. It has been estimated that a staggering 80 per cent of the men forced into slave labour by the Japanese died during their captivity.

Some of the British POWs in Europe also faced severe levels of abuse as they were re-classed as concentration camp inmates.

It is unclear how many Allied men were forced to work as slaves for the Nazis. Most of these men were not Jewish. Many of them had escaped from other POW camps or had worked with underground resistance units. Their actions led the Nazis to re-categorize them as political prisoners, which meant they lost their POW status and, therefore, the rights afforded to them under the Geneva Convention. Various British soldiers were dispatched to concentration camps which included Buchenwald, Belsen and Theresienstadt.

I have researched and sourced various documents compiled by war crimes investigators. These papers contained the testimonies of hundreds of British POWs sent to E715 Auschwitz and were collated for the Nuremburg Trials.

The men who provided these witness statements were interviewed between 1945 and 1947 when their memories would still have been reasonably 'fresh'. Their statements are included within this book and broadly concur with the recollections provided by Brian Bishop, Arthur Gifford-England and Doug Bond.

It is unclear why the Nazis established a prisoner of war facility alongside the main concentration camp at Auschwitz, and it is not known why Brian and his compatriots were sent to this particular facility. Also, it is something of a mystery why their story has remained unrevealed for so many years. The British Government has always accepted these men were sent to E715 Auschwitz. The majority of them have never received any compensation for their ordeal.

Some of the survivors suffered with post-traumatic disorder as a result of watching the constant violence and death happening around them. Few people seemed interested in the story of these remarkable men on their return to this country. This book seeks to redress that balance and sets out to record a forgotten part of our history by utilizing the memories of the few surviving British men who witnessed mass murder in Auschwitz. This is their story.

1

Background

Brian Bishop was about to embark on a train journey that would change his life forever. He thought his transport, from a POW camp in Nazi Germany to a new camp in Poland, would be like any other prison transfer.

As he boarded the cattle truck, he was completely oblivious that his final destination would be to a place called Auschwitz – somewhere that few outside of the hierarchy of Nazi Germany had ever heard of. It was a name that meant nothing to Brian but would become synonymous with mass murder for generations to come. He would not face death as he was not a Jew or a political prisoner. As a POW, Brian Bishop's safety was 'guaranteed' under the terms of the Geneva Convention.

Brian was the eldest of eight children and was born in Portslade in Sussex in 1920. His father had served in the army for twelve years and Brian wanted to follow in his footsteps. The young corporal was only 19 years old when war broke out in 1939. He was one of the last soldiers to be evacuated from the beaches of Dunkirk in June 1940.

He was sent back into service against Rommel's troops in Africa before being captured by the Germans in 1942. Rommel himself apologized to Brian and the other British troops

Brian Bishop, past and present

for handing them over to the Italians. Their treatment of POWs was renowned for being poor. Eventually, Brian was sent to a camp in Germany whereupon he heard that food rations were better if you volunteered for a 'working party'. He duly did so and soon found himself en route to his new POW camp in Poland.

He would be sent to a small facility on the outskirts of the Nazis' largest death camp. Auschwitz was set to become the largest centre for the destruction of the Jews and more than one million people would die at this location. Approximately six million Jews would be murdered during the course of the Holocaust.

Doug Bond's route to Auschwitz was similar as he was also captured in North Africa. Born in Goldhawk Road in Shepherd's Bush on 8 November 1918, Doug joined the Post Office as an engineer before signing up to the Army in 1939.

They trained him in Devon, Kent and Somerset before he boarded a ship in Glasgow, in May 1941, where he was transported with a whole division to North Africa. The journey took eight weeks and their mission, on arrival, was to fight against Rommel's troops. He was captured near Tobruk, on 1 June 1942, and he remembers that as a 22-year-old he was frightened as he simply did not know what was going to happen to him or his comrades.

'We were under gunfire for three days as the Germans were shelling our line. I was in a dugout when they broke through

Doug Bond, past and present. Top left, *1939.* Top right, *in Crediton, Devon, 1939 – Doug is on the left*

and we were marched into their custody. We wondered what was going to happen to us and we didn't know if we were going to get home.' He was also sent to a POW camp in Italy before being transported to Auschwitz.

Arthur Gifford-England was born in Kingston St Mary (near Taunton) in Somerset on 1 August, 1919. He studied as an apprentice in carpentry before joining the Army 'out of a sense of patriotism' in January 1940. He became a Royal Engineer, before being sent to Egypt in the same year, to fight Rommel's troops.

Like Doug, Arthur was also captured in Tobruk. He recalls 'feeling nothing' when he had a German 'pointing a gun at him' but remembers that he soon 'felt relief' that the fighting had finally stopped. That relief was soon replaced with fear of what was going to happen to him and his fellow soldiers.

He was sent to a camp in Italy where he was treated roughly. He also spent time in a German POW camp which 'had mud up to your eyeballs'. He was subsequently sent to E715 Auschwitz.

'They never told us where we were going, they just told us that we were being sent to a working camp. I was glad to leave that POW camp as we thought we were going to a smaller place which would mean better facilities.'

These three men's lives were to be changed for ever as they would become key witnesses to extreme brutality. These young men were among hundreds of other British prisoners

Arthur Gifford-England, past and present

of war who would shortly meet the victims of the concentration camps. Brian, Doug and Arthur would become among the few Allied servicemen to witness the events surrounding the Holocaust.

2

Cattle Trucks to Auschwitz

As many of the death camps (including Auschwitz) were sited in the eastern part of Hitler's empire, the need to move millions of innocent people to their deaths was a major exercise in logistics for the Nazis. Strong transport links, therefore, were seen as vitally important for the Final Solution. The Nazis established a colossal network of railway lines spanning Europe. It meant Jews would be crammed into cattle trucks and spend days heading towards the death camps.

The majority of the captured British soldiers also needed to be moved from their camps in Germany or Italy to their new location. Their POW camp was simply termed E715 Auschwitz. It was a name that meant nothing to the young British men on the trains but today is synonymous with mass murder.

Like the Jews, the soldiers were loaded onto cattle trucks and journeyed across Europe for hundreds of miles. Their transportation, however, was far less crowded than the Jewish transports and the Nazis sometimes provided a small amount of food for the soldiers. The British were also unaware of their final destiny – or what they were about to witness.

Doug Bond was taken prisoner by the Germans in the latter part of 1943. He had been imprisoned in Italy before joining hundreds of other men in ten separate cattle trucks on a seven-day journey from Florence to Auschwitz. Each carriage held 40 British soldiers. The train stopped at night to give the driver and the guards a break. The POWs, however, remained inside the carriages – with practically no food and very little water.

'When we stopped at night, they occasionally supplied us with a sour cabbage soup which had been boiled over and over again,' says Doug. 'We got that once or twice during our seven days. We didn't get a lot as there were about five hundred men in the whole train and so they had to ration us.'

Wartime documents reveal how one group of Allied POWs were re-classified as concentration camp inmates and subsequently sent to Buchenwald. They were unaware of their true destination as the Nazis had told them they were being taken to another 'prisoner of war camp'.

In one report, Squadron Leader P. J. Lamason (RNZAF) explained how 168 men (including himself and a group of Americans) were 'forced into box cars' on 15 August 1944. His report estimated that each truck held 80 to 90 men 'which hardly allowed seating room for everyone'.

He noted conditions became 'extremely unpleasant' due to both the summer's warmth and the lack of proper ventilation (there were two small windows at each end of the car).[1]

In a separate account of the same journey, Flight Lieutenant

Edgar Jackson (RAF) remembered how the Allied prisoners were joined by French inmates. Together they were 'crowded into box carriages'. He estimated that some of the cars contained nearly one hundred people (including women).[2]

After two arduous days, in appalling conditions, the train stopped. The guards forced the men and women to march two to three miles to another set of cattle trucks. They beat a number of prisoners during the transfer and took six British and American officers hostage. They threatened to execute any POW who attempted to escape.

In his post-war affidavit, Jackson explained how conditions in the second train were even worse for the Allied prisoners. The truck was coated in lime, 'which added to our distress', and by now some of the POWs were very sick with a few of the men suffering from dysentery. Their journey would last another three days.

One Canadian flight lieutenant suffered an epileptic fit – no medical help was made available to him.

The 75 men in Jackson's truck were issued with approximately ten Red Cross parcels. Each package was shared between seven men.

The Germans also gave them a loaf and a small tin of sausages. A canister of water was also placed in the carriage which was 'two feet high and one foot in diameter'. His affidavit noted this container was 'filled once during the five nights and six days on the train. It was very hot and the prisoners suffered much thirst.'[3]

On his journey to E715 Auschwitz, Doug remembers that there were no toilets and the soldiers were forced to relieve themselves in the corner of the truck. The smell became unbearable. He says, 'It was uncomfortable and you didn't know what was going to happen – but we survived the week.'

Brian cannot remember how long the journey from his POW camp in Nazi Germany to E715 Auschwitz lasted. He does, however, recall conditions in the similar carriages which were used when he was transported from Italy to Germany. 'On the side of the trucks I think it said eight cattle and there was about 20 of us on a truck. There must have been six to eight trucks.'

'All we had on the truck was an old galvanized bath and once it got filled up [they had been using it as a toilet] the rocking meant it overflowed – all over the place. Some of the chaps had knives and we were able to cut holes in the floor so we managed to relieve ourselves through the holes in the truck.'

The journey to E715 Auschwitz was different as the trucks were more crowded and there was no bath to act as a temporary toilet. 'You couldn't lie down as there were so many people in one truck,' says Brian. 'You might have been able to stretch your legs but you would probably kick someone in the head. The Jews were packed more tightly. They were in similar trucks to us and I think all they could do was stand there. They couldn't even sit down.'

Arthur Gifford-England's journey from Germany to Poland

was 'rough'. He remembers the soldiers' bewilderment on seeing the main gates to Auschwitz as their train rumbled past the huge complex. Jewish transports would pass into this section of the camp whereupon people would be divided into the groups of those who would live and those who would die. Arthur remembers it was late at night when they passed the main complex. The whole area was lit up and the men in the truck 'wondered what the hell was going on'.

They were concerned about their own fate and had been supplied with little food or water during their journey. They could not see much from the small open window which was covered in barbed wire. When they finally left the truck, they were simply grateful to have survived. The men then walked, in darkness, for two to three miles to the new POW camp.

Their relief at finally arriving at the E715 Auschwitz soon turned to horror as they realized what was happening around them. Doug remembers, 'We didn't know where we were until a couple of days after we had first arrived there. We were being marched out of the camp to go to work and that's when we came across the Jewish people in their pyjamas. We started to ask questions: Who are these people and where did they come from?'

3

Recollections

In 2006, Brian Bishop showed me the two impressive tattoos of women which he sported on his arms. Neither came from a professional tattooist (one has her head pointing the wrong way). Nor did Brian pay cash for them. Instead the work cost him 20 cigarettes. Nicotine was the standard currency at E715 Auschwitz. It was a Northumberland man who sketched the pictures onto tracing paper and pressed it onto Brian's arms. Another man had to use a needle to mark the area with indelible ink (the prisoners did not have access to any specialist tattooing equipment). It has acted as a permanent reminder for a part of Brian's life that he would have preferred to forget.

He arrived at E715 Auschwitz in October 1943. For the next year and three months, Brian became prisoner 31113. He was incarcerated alongside hundreds of other British prisoners. First, they were housed in a camp on the edge of the complex (with a field nearby) and then they were subsequently sited in a camp opposite the massive industrial factory of IG Farben.

The Nazis believed Brian and his fellow soldiers would play an important role in building and developing IG Farben, which was vital for the Third Reich's war effort. Prior to 1939, it was a major producer of both rubber and fuel. As soon as hostilities started, there was a tremendous pressure on the company to meet the rising demands of the German Army, Navy and Air Force. New sites needed to be found and quickly established. The Germans soon decided to use Auschwitz as a key producer of its wartime needs and building work began. Brian estimates a third of the complex had been completed by the end of 1943.

The decision to place this key facility in Poland was partly due to the plentiful supply of concentration camp inmates. They were seen as cheap labour for the Nazi war machine, and the British POWs would work alongside them. Its location away from the front line made it safer from air attacks. It was an assumption which would ultimately lead to the deaths of 38 British POWs towards the end of the war.

The development of the IG Farben factory boosted the local economy by drawing upon a workforce consisting of people from the surrounding population. The local workers proved to be a vital lifeline for the hungry British soldiers as they could smuggle food supplies into the camp.

The rules of the Geneva Convention were largely ignored in E715. In one case, British POWs argued with a Nazi commander that they would not work for the German war effort as it was against international law. The Nazis simply responded with threats and argued the Convention did not apply to POWs. The British were told they were working for 'an international firm' which meant they were 'not working for the Germans'.[1]

Frederick Davison was assigned to carry pipes from one part of the complex to another. After the war, he explained to investigators that the POWs initially believed IG Farben was a paint factory. They were shocked to learn that they would be helping the Germans: 'When we protested that this was war work which prisoners didn't have to perform, the German commandant who was a member of the German Army, pounded on the table and pointing to his revolver said, "This is my Geneva Convention." '[2]

IG Farben's management stood trial after the war. One of them tried to argue that the company was simply unaware of their responsibilities under international law. He stated, 'I do not recall . . . that it was not permissible under the Geneva or the Hague Conventions respectively to employ prisoners of war in armament undertakings.'[3]

Rules on allowing POWs access to regular Red Cross parcels, however, were not overlooked. On some occasions these deliveries were not wholeheartedly reliable, but they undoubtedly became a lifesaving factor in the POWs' diet.

It is very hard to put an exact figure on the number of British POWs at E715 as estimates vary according to different accounts and testimonies.

John Pascoe (Manchester) arrived in Auschwitz in October 1943. He gave evidence to the Nuremburg Trials in 1947 and wrote, 'There were about 1500 British prisoners of war at

Auschwitz with me and there were many thousands of Russians, Poles and other nationalities as well as concentration camp inmates working there at the time.'[4] John Adkin (London) arrived at the camp in September 1943. He estimated that there were a total of 900 POWs.[5]

Norbert Wollheim was a Jew arrested in Berlin on 8 March 1943 with his wife and his three-year-old son. He was separated from his family when he arrived at Auschwitz. He never saw them again. In his post-war affidavit, he remembered the British prisoners who 'openly confessed their sympathy for us'.[6] He estimated that a total of 1200 British POWs were brought into the camp in the autumn of 1943. Brian would have been among these men.

Charles Coward acted as the British POWs' Red Cross Trustee. He concurred with Wollheim's initial estimates[7] but stated that six hundred men were moved to Heydebreck and Blechhammer camps at the start of 1944. It meant around six hundred British prisoners were left behind during the closing stages of the war. These men started their march to freedom on 21 January 1945. By then, they had endured regular beatings, one of their comrades had been shot dead, another had been stabbed and dozens had died in an Allied aerial bombing. For the surviving men, the long-term psychological torment would leave emotional scars that lasted far longer than the physical ones.

When Brian and his fellow POWs arrived they knew nothing of the Jews or Auschwitz. They marched along a road to their new living quarters – placed around two miles from the crematoria. Brian recalls catching a glimpse of concentration camp inmates for the first time: 'We could see people through the wire and they were carrying this pole and the tall ones were on the end carrying it and the little ones were in the middle which was so silly as they were just hanging on and were staggering all over the place and – of course – they had pyjama suits on which were grey and blue stripes.' It was not until the British were settled into their work that they met the Jews and discovered the true extent and nature of the Nazis' killing machine. Charlie Coward wrote in his affidavit that the prisoners would hear five or six shootings a week from the nearby concentration camp.

'It took a long time for us to understand the situation,' says Doug Bond. 'But when we saw these blokes walking around in pyjamas we realized it was a concentration camp. We automatically thought [that, as Prisoners of War] we were going to get home and we couldn't afford to think of their fate, nor could we think in a negative way. But, at the time, we couldn't help them and you just felt sorry for them – especially in winter, when they had nothing to keep them warm. In those days the number one rule was to look after yourselves; we did try to feed them the odd bits when we could, and when the SS weren't looking, but you had to be on your guard when you did.'

The POW camp was a mixed blessing for the British sol-

Hut 12, E715 Auschwitz. Arthur Gifford-England is in the back row, second to left

diers. Many of these men had experienced poor conditions during their imprisonment in Italy. The facilities in E715 were arguably better in certain respects than in Mussolini's camps. For instance, one of the Italian camps had an improvised toilet consisting of a bar over a trench. Passers-by would laugh at the prisoners as they relieved themselves in the open air. In Auschwitz, a roof protected their dignity and sheltered them from the elements.

Brian and his compatriots were originally housed on the 'outskirts' of Auschwitz. They were moved to a newer camp in February 1944. It was located directly opposite the IG Farben factory. They noticed a marked improvement in the sanitary conditions. Gone were bars over pits – they were replaced with holes in wooden planks. This 'new' British camp even had showers. Brian recalls there was a repair room for clothes and shoes together with a small library which consisted of a collection of up to a hundred books – including a copy of Hitler's *Mein Kampf*.

Brian remembers how one young man arrived late for work. One of the guards confronted the POW over his poor timekeeping. The British soldier explained he had been delayed because he had been 'busy reading' *Mein Kampf*. The German merely laughed and let the Englishman off.

The POWs generally received a more regular supply of Red Cross parcels. In Italy, Red Cross parcels would be shared between two to three people. At E715 Auschwitz, the POWs would often receive a single parcel each. Such a 'luxury' would allow them to trade the contents with the local people who worked in the factory – often for eggs and bread which would be smuggled back to the POWs' huts.

The parcels would weigh ten pounds and would come from either England or Canada. In his unpublished written account, Doug Bond (prisoner number 32851) stated Canadian parcels would contain a tin of bully beef or spam, a packet of biscuits (he remembered these were similar to crackers but were a lot thicker), butter, coffee, sugar, powered milk which was called Klim (milk spelt backwards) and a small bar of soap.

English parcels contained less milk but the loss was compensated by tinned meats and vegetables together with puddings. Doug recalled the Geneva Convention stated they were supposed to be fed standard rations. The Germans failed in their obligation.

Cigarettes were sent by family members via the Red Cross and the packages became vital to British morale and strength. One 'Next of Kin' parcel to Brian (dated 22 December 1944) included a towel, two vests, toothpaste and a toothbrush. Brian would write to his mother asking her to send him tobacco so he could barter with the Germans and the Poles in the factory. She was reluctant as she disagreed with the habit. When he did have cigarettes then he could exchange them for eggs, pork and even alcohol – before illicitly taking these items back to his barracks.

Other Red Cross packages came from Scotland. They included tea, oatmeal and biscuits which Brian remembers made 'good porridge'. The parcels from New Zealand included raisins, honey and jam. In 1944, the POWs received an English Christmas parcel where the food ranged from a Yorkshire pudding and custard powder through to a twelve-ounce Christmas cake. It also contained honey, sardines, milk chocolate and baked beans.

As the British were guarded by members of the German Army (as opposed to the SS) smuggling 'offences' were often overlooked. If they were caught then the 'contraband' would often be confiscated, although harsher penalties were not uncommon – a risk Brian and others were willing to take.

If someone was caught breaking the rules then the Geneva Convention would not necessarily act as their protector.

Brian notes that there were small cells in the camp where British soldiers would be sent for 'small misdemeanours' which included 'trading with civilians in the factory'.

'We used to see SS but never heard of SS guarding British troops,' he says. 'It would seem to be quite a waste of time. I think it was beneath their dignity to do it quite honestly. Most of the soldiers that looked after us were either unfit for duty or had been to the battlefield and had got injured and were unfit for fighting.' But that did not mean that the SS would not strike British troops. Arthur Gifford-England remembers that 'to the SS it did not matter who was guarding you, if they didn't think you were working hard enough then they would hit you'.

Brian recalls the SS would sometimes come into the British camp to search for contraband. Fortunately for him, he carefully hid his cigarettes in various cavities around the hut.

There were around 80 men to a hut which was divided into four rooms, with 20 people in each room. The British occupied around five to six huts and each one had a clear area in the middle where there was a table.

Heating was a major issue. In Poland, temperatures would drop to 30 degrees below zero. The prisoners' quarters contained 'hot' water pipes which ran the entire length of the huts. The heating did not always work as former POWs recall how icicles would form on the beams and how clothes would be frozen solid. Allied prisoners in Italy had no heating at all. They would often use wooden slats from their beds to light fires and they would burn charcoal in cups to heat water for tea or coffee.

The huts at E715 Auschwitz were made of wood with asbestos insulating the inner frame. Italian camps were mainly stone buildings which made the summer heat more bearable but it also meant the POWs would feel the seasonal cold.

In Auschwitz they witnessed a daily barrage of brutality against Jewish inmates. It was a desperate situation for the British soldiers. In his affidavit, Charles Coward recalled how concentration camp inmates were 'beaten on the slightest provocation and often without any provocation at all'. He recounted how, on one occasion, the POWs witnessed civilian employees abuse six inmates by beating them 'with pieces of iron and wood for not doing their work properly'. Coward was so shocked at this event that he used his position, as the key contact point between the POWs and the Nazis, to complain to a German officer. He explained that such events upset the morale of the British prisoners. The German replied 'that the inmates deserved it and that if they did not get beaten, they would be hard to control'.[8]

Frederick Davison recorded his affidavit for Nuremburg in 1947. He said that he witnessed murder being 'committed on four or five different occasions'. He also stated that the inmates would be murdered 'in the streets of the factory grounds. I have seen the bodies themselves hundreds of times'. The inmates would collapse on a daily basis and he would watch as 'every night they used to be carried back to the camp on planks of wood'.[9]

Robert Ferris recalled that the POWs could hear 'shooting going on at the camp on a number of different times'.[10] Arthur Gifford-England remembers seeing the incessant brutality against the Jews, even witnessing inmates killing each other as the Capos turned on their own. The Capos were effectively 'foremen' who (despite being concentration camp victims themselves) were renowned for being especially brutal towards the others around them. In return, they would receive better rations and a 'better' life.

The relentless violence meant, despite the hardships of Mussolini's camps, Brian would have preferred to have remained in Italy rather than languishing in Poland.

The British huts were a mere 200 yards from the concentration camp and the British would listen to the Jewish orchestra as they played classical music to try to relieve tension as the inmates were marched to the factory. For these people there were no Red Cross parcels, and hundreds of them would sleep on shelves which would stretch across the length of the huts.

Brian remembers on one occasion returning to Camp E715 to see bodies hanging from a nearby gallows. 'They were in the middle of a field,' he recalls. 'There were four ropes on a makeshift gallows with four bodies hanging from them. No one seemed bothered that they were there; it was one of those things that happened and there's nothing we could do about it. It was no different to someone being shot down in the factory.' Placards stating the victims' 'crime' had been placed around their necks. Being 150 yards away, the British were unable to read the notices but it is likely that the death penalty had been instigated for one of a number of minor 'offences'.

There was no escaping death in Auschwitz. Brian is still haunted by the terrible smell of the crematoria, 'if the wind was blowing in the wrong direction then you could smell this awful, sickly smell. That upset me more than anything I think. For the smell alone I would have preferred to stay in the Italian POW camps.'

It was not only the British who were sickened by the smell. Some of the Nazis also had problems trying to cope with it. Christian Schneider was a senior official in IG Farben. In his post-war affidavit, he stated that the crematoriums' chimneys could be seen from the factory. He visited the site on two separate occasions. He remembered factory officials complained about the 'terrible smell' from the cremations.[11]

Soon after arriving at E715 Auschwitz, Brian and the others were put to work for the German war effort – in direct violation of the Geneva Convention. When asked what work the men did in civilian life, the British explained they were unable to help the Nazis in building their factory. The soldiers said their skills laid elsewhere – one even stated that he was a professional lion tamer.

Brian was truthful and explained he was a clerk. He was tasked with work on the railways where he picked up flanges and carried items to help build the gasworks for IG Farben. Like most of the men, he made no effort to work for the Germans who seemed to tolerate the British 'laissez-faire' attitude. Many of the men who guarded the POWs were ineffective as they had either been injured in the war or were too old to carry out their duties properly. It meant security surrounding the British was surprisingly lax. 'If you thought they weren't taking any notice,' says Brian, 'then you could just clear off for half an hour and if anybody said anything when you came back then you would just say you had been to the toilet.'

British morale was buoyed with news of Allied victories. The information supposedly came from radio sets secretly housed within the British camp. It is unclear if these receivers actually existed or if they were 'created' to help bolster British resolve. Arthur Gifford-England remembers how it was rumoured that some of the British had managed to build basic radios. He never saw one but had been told that someone would listen to BBC News for half an hour every night. The news would be disseminated the following day. Jewish inmate Norbert Wollheim[12] spoke English and would regularly try to talk with the POWs. In his post-war affidavit, he writes: 'The POWs were able to keep me informed daily of the BBC News from London, for they had a secret receiving set in their barracks, and I, on my part, translated for them the German Army news bulletins I heard.' After the war, Charlie Coward wrote that the POWs at Auschwitz would 'get radio broadcasts from the outside speaking about the gassings and burnings at Auschwitz. I recall one of these broadcasts was by Anthony Eden himself.'[13]

The news of Allied victories may have lifted morale, but the day-to-day fight for survival continued as the POWs continued to work in the plant. Doug Bond recalls the men nicknamed IG Farben the 'Queen Mary' because its sheer size and proliferation of funnels gave it the appearance of the Cunard White Star's ocean liner. Brian remembers the men's bemusement at discovering the girders for the new factory came from Middlesbrough.

Two British servicemen worked as steeplejacks. It had been their pre-war work and they felt it was good practice for them. One of them fell from a chimney and became badly injured.

The IG Farben plant, Auschwitz

Doug was put to work moving acetylene bottles which the welders would use. He worked alongside six other men who would replenish the spent bottles with new ones. It was a laborious task which (during summer months) would start at six in the morning and finally end at five in the evening.

His team and other POWs soon set about trying to sabotage the German war effort. They would try to leave the valves open on the full bottles in the evening – by morning they would be empty. This small act of defiance went largely unnoticed but it cost the Nazis time (and money) as the bottles would have to be refilled.

In other parts of the camp the British were made to lay pipes for a new factory. They would try to fill the pipes with mud and dirt – another small example of resistance to the Nazi war machine.

Arthur Gifford-England remembers that the British mantra was to perform 'the minimum amount of work and the maximum amount of damage'. They effectively engaged in sabotage tactics whilst being careful not to arouse suspicion. Arthur remembers how they would exchange labels on trucks destined for the Russian Front with those on other trains. The resulting confusion meant German troops would receive paint instead of bullets.

He also recounts how a group of POWs were tasked with laying an electric cable. One of them stuck a pickaxe through it. The supply failed when the Nazis flipped the switch.

Arthur remembers his compatriots laughed at the result. The Nazis took no action against them.

Not all 'acts of defiance' went unpunished. During winter, the temperature within the factory itself would often drop to minus ten – outside it was even colder. It made working conditions extremely harsh, particularly as the POWs were never supplied with proper protective clothing.

'You could always tell the ones who worked outside because they would have patches on their knees,' says Brian. 'We used to get these old big tins and then find odd bits of wood lying around – there was always plenty – which we would burn in the tin. You used to stand as close to it as you could and the knees of your trousers would get so dry and crispy that as soon as you moved at all, they would split. You could always tell someone who worked outside the factory as they would have mended their trousers with these patches around the knees.'

Such cold would mean unprotected skin would be instantly frozen to a metal object if it came into contact with it. Bad weather conditions, however, could not stand in the way of the German war effort, which was then failing. Brian recalls their first commandant at Camp E715 was a man called Rittler. At the end of the war, Allied intelligence and war crimes investigators tried to hunt the Nazi down for war crimes against Allied prisoners. Rittler had meted out his own punishment for British acts of defiance and was accused of fatally shooting one British corporal (named in post-war documents as Reynolds). The British prisoner's 'crime' had been to refuse an order to 'climb 70 feet up girders in the deep cold of the 1943 winter'. Reynolds thought he would freeze to the metal and argued it was not safe as the Nazis had refused to provide him with any proper clothing.[14]

Other witnesses accused another Nazi (Benno Franz) of the shooting. Franz was despised by the POWs who knew that he had stabbed a British soldier (Private Campbell) in a separate incident. After the war, they explained the assault happened because the POW helped a Polish girl carry a 'pail of soup'.[15]

The British soldiers' reaction to Reynolds' death was a forced resignation – there was little they could do to help their fallen comrade. A few men planned to drop concrete blocks (from girders) as the guilty Nazis walked underneath. The plan was never executed.

Brian believes the shooting incident led to Rittler being dispatched to the Russian Front by his superiors. He recalls how the commandant would fire his gun through the British huts to ensure prisoners were out of their bunks, on parade and ready to go to work at the crack of dawn. On one occasion, this performance resulted in one British man being injured by a stray bullet as he lay on his bed.

One POW used humour to defuse Rittler's notorious temper. The Nazi had caught the soldier trying to smuggle food back into the camp. Brian remembers how the man had found a duck at the lake which was next to the IG Farben complex. He killed it and then strapped it loosely around his neck so it swung between his legs – a heavy coat hiding his secret. On returning to the camp, he was randomly searched and the animal was quickly discovered. Rittler demanded to know how the man had obtained the 'illegal' food.

The soldier explained he had been walking around the lake when he came across a very aggressive duck. The creature, he continued, had tried to attack him. He explained that killing it was an act of 'self-defence'. Brian recalls that the Nazi laughed so much that the Englishman was not only 'let off' but was also allowed to keep the duck.

The prisoner was fortunate as an unknown number of British POWs were sent to a 'hard labour' camp for such misdemeanours. Other 'offences' included damaging Nazi equipment. Many men spent several weeks toiling in a quarry or underground in the coal mines at nearby Sosnowitz (Sosnowiec). There are various accounts relating to the poor conditions suffered by British POWs as they worked below ground. Their task was to try to dig out and haul the coal to the surface.

Eric Stamp had been a sapper in the Royal Engineers and was sent to Sosnowitz in Christmas 1943 having been captured three years earlier. He recounted his experience to war crime investigators. Stamp was put to work in the mines which were around 700 feet deep. The Germans needed the ore for their war effort and the British struggled with the exceptionally poor conditions. Some of the men sustained broken arms and legs as they laboured to replace rotting props. On average, they would work between 12 to 14 hours a day in the flooded mine-shafts. In January and February 1944, the POWs were forced to work every day of the week. They were provided with no additional rations and their daily allowance consisted of 500 grams of bread, one pound of potatoes and a thin watery soup.

After the war, investigators attempted to locate the mine manager to prosecute him over breaches of the Geneva Convention. It is unclear if they successfully found him (or not) as many Nazi war criminals simply vanished after 1945. Stamp's testimony became the crucial piece of evidence used to build a case by the authorities. Their argument was simple: 'Conditions [in the pit] were bad, and for these the accused was responsible.'[16]

In his post-war affidavit, Charlie Coward also notes how 'a large number of our lads were sent to Sosnowitz to the Straflager for not working hard enough or for refusing to do the work ordered'.[17]

In a separate incident, one British prisoner was shot in the Pothen salt mine (Germany) as he argued against the Nazis who wanted him to work on a Sunday. Post-war reports explained how a row with a guard led to Private Robert Clarkson being shot 'through the head'.[18] Post-war papers noted how the guilty party was a decorated Nazi – who wore a medal for his service on the Russian front.

Fortunately, Brian was never sent to Sosnowitz or the Pothen salt mine. Despite the risks of hard labour, he and the others were still willing to take risks to smuggle goods back to the camp. It was possible, but for a price. He struck up a symbiotic relationship with one of the guards at the factory. They would search the POWs as they entered and left each day. Once he had obtained food from civilian employees at IG Farben then he would simply slip into the queue where the amiable guard would 'search' him and let him pass through unhindered.

Later Brian would repay the favour by providing the guard with cigarettes from his Red Cross parcels. Being guarded by *Wehmacht* soldiers had advantages for the British. At one point, he even managed to smuggle ten eggs and two loaves of bread back to the huts. The Jews, however, were guarded by fanatical SS officers who would sadistically deal out harsh penalties with little or no warning.

One 32-year-old Polish Jew (Isreal Majzlik) received 15 lashes from the cane and was also forced to work underground for an undetermined amount of time. His crime was to be caught by the SS taking an 'illicit' break. He was simply sitting down, smoking and talking with an English POW.[19]

The British quickly became aware of what was happening to the Jews – not just by the smell from the crematoria but also from the inmates themselves. Some could speak English and would talk with the British. Brian remembers, 'They used to come in and one of them was missing and you used to say, "Where's so and so?" and they used to say, "Gone for a shower," and you used to say, "Without a soap and towel," and they just used to nod their heads and you knew then that they had gone to the gas chambers.'

On another occasion, Brian became friendly with a French Jew whose clothes were torn. The British corporal offered to help mend them by supplying the former lawyer with some knitted materials. Unfortunately, the Nazis found out and the Jew was taken away. 'They put him into a punishment box,' says Brian, who never saw one of these small rooms, but later heard about it from other concentration camp inmates. 'From all accounts these were boxes that were only about two feet high and so you would have to crouch with your knees up and they used to keep you there as a punishment for the whole day. I never saw him again so I don't know if he got moved to a different working party or if he went to the gas chambers.'

Such brutality was commonplace and the British tried to help by giving the Jews some of the meagre rations supplied by the Nazis. It was seen as an act of kindness remembered by many concentration camp victims after the war. The food, however, was simply inedible for the British POWs.

'At Auschwitz, we used to get bread issued at dinnertime and we would get cabbage soup down in the works which we never ate,' recounts Brian. 'We always gave it to the Jews because it stank so badly you just couldn't drink it. I don't know what they put in it, I think it was all the rotten waste they had from cooking. It was all the outside cabbage leaves and all the rubbish left over that they would put in the soup.

Take the lid off it and it really stank so we used to give it to the Jews and they were really thankful.'

Doug records the care needed when giving the soup to Jewish inmates, 'If the SS spotted us offering soup to the Jews then they would kick the bucket over and threaten to shoot. We were glad that we were guarded by ordinary troops.' He remembers how the sour cabbage soup would make him feel sick.

Despite the Red Cross parcels and the illicit supplies from the factory, there simply was not enough food for all the men and it became a constant source of tension for the soldiers. In his unpublished post-war account entitled 'Life behind Barbed Wire', Doug Bond wrote about one of his comrades who gave away his false set of teeth for a loaf of bread – then borrowed them back so he could eat it. He recounted how one man slept with a loaf tucked under his chin. On waking up he discovered the ends had been cut off and eaten by another hungry British inmate.

Brian remembers they received bread and sometimes 'a pink substance that looked like semolina'. The Nazis also provided them with a 'cheese that looked like a fish cake, tasted of fish and smelt awful'.

By the start of 1944, the situation in E715 Auschwitz was dire. Doug recounts how the camp reached a low point when they had run out of cigarettes and Red Cross parcels. His compatriots ended up lying in bed 'too weak to stand on their feet. We would just lie there, all day, thinking of food, which

The 'England' football team, Auschwitz E715. Doug Bond is at the centre in the back row. Charlie Coward has his hands on Doug's shoulders

we did not have, not speaking out loud on this subject as it would cause arguments and fights.'

The one escape for the POWs was football. Sunday was their rest day and four teams were selected from hundreds of men – each eleven-man team would be made up of either Welsh, English or Scottish players. Doug would play in goal and one of the German factory foremen would often try to sneak him an extra half a loaf of bread to keep his strength up for the matches.

Hundreds of people would come to watch. Prisoners and local people (who worked in the factory) made up the spectators. The event gave the British a much needed morale lift and a clear respite from the horrors they were witnessing on a daily basis. The field was outside of their camp's perimeters and a clear mile from the concentration camps.

Their kit was supplied by the Red Cross and consisted of shirts, shorts and football boots. Each team had their own colours – reds for Welsh, blues for Scots and white shirts for the English players. The matches could only take place during the summer and only if there were enough guards to man the event. During winter, it simply wasn't safe to spend any unnecessary time outside as the temperatures dropped well below freezing.

The majority of fixtures appear to have taken place in 1944. Doug estimates that he played around half a dozen games and believes that, as the Nazis realized they were losing the war, they became more hospitable towards the idea of regular football tournaments. He also noticed they became less hostile and less belligerent towards the POWs.

A large running track lined the football field and the British would sometimes race against each other. Brian remembers one occasion where 'we decided to see how many times we could run around it. Some blokes managed to run around it once or twice but we had a South African chap who was still running about an hour after everyone else had finished.'

The British also played bridge. Brian was in charge of his hut which consisted of 20 men – ten of them would play regular card games. Work would often last from dawn to dusk and it would sometimes give the men a chance to unwind in the evenings or on their day off.

They even staged their own version of Sweeny Todd. Eleven men, including Arthur Gifford-England, took part in the production which was designed to raise morale. A poster was produced for the event. It included credits for costumes, lighting and props. The small-scale performance was staged during the evening of 2 December 1944 and lasted for around an hour. The Germans attended and a censor sat in the front row. Arthur, who played the part of a policeman, remembers that the official's role was to ensure that the British did not make derogatory remarks about Adolf Hitler. The cast were also banned from singing 'God Save the King'. Instead they decided on a rendition of 'Land of Hope and Glory'. Arthur recalls that two burly POWs sat either side of the censor. When the cast began singing, the two men pushed against the censor and forced him to stand.

Different men handled the stress of daily life in E715 in different ways. Before the war, Arthur enjoyed gardening. During work in the factory, his hand was crushed and the injury meant he could no longer carry out manual work. He found a shovel and approached Charlie Coward to ask for help in making a small garden. Coward had been captured in May 1940 whilst serving with the Royal Artillery. In his post-war affidavit, he stated he was 'able to move around without too much difficulty' as he was a Red Cross Trustee and 'liaison man' between the POWs and the Nazis. Coward used his bartering skills (and cigarettes) to obtain plants from the nearby town of Oswiecim. Following the spring of 1944,

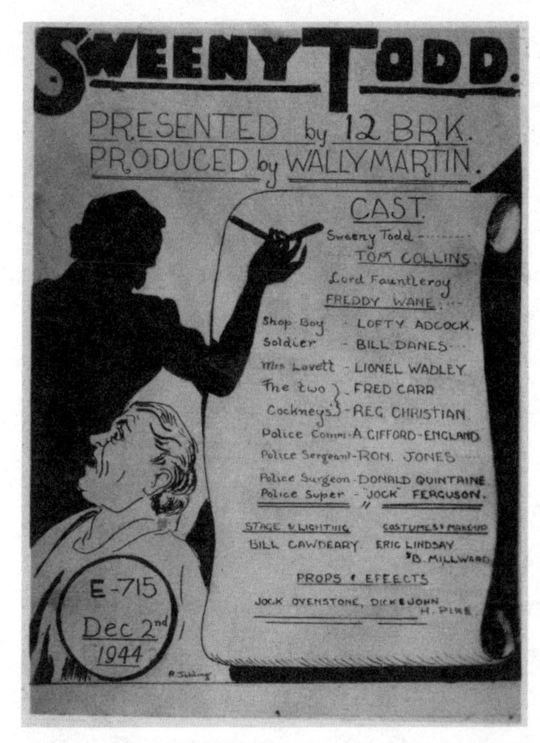

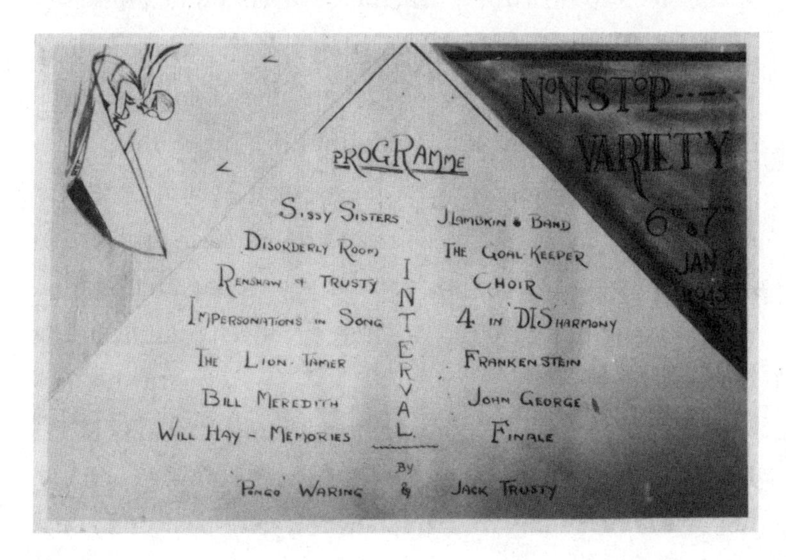

Top, *the Sweeny Todd programme.* Bottom, *'Variety Show' programme, dated 6–7 January 1945, E715 Auschwitz*

Arthur set about transforming a small patch of land next to the POWs' huts.

He planted tomatoes and flowers into an area roughly six feet by six feet. No other POW (or inmate) had made a garden and it gave Arthur something to focus on. He also saw it as his own act of defiance against the Nazi regime. He would use the cesspit as a good source of manure. But the tomatoes never bore any fruit as the garden only lasted for a few months. It was next to the concentration camp and he witnessed acts of cruelty on a daily basis.

He still recalls the day his garden was destroyed by the American bombing run of 5 August 1944 which resulted in the death of 38 British soldiers. Their bodies remain in a war cemetery in Poland. The tragedy had a profound effect on morale. The men had been running to take cover in a bomb shelter next to their camp when it received a direct hit.

Significantly, the bombing happened on a Sunday morning when the POWs were relaxing in their huts. Doug still clearly recalls the events. 'It was a beautiful day. There was a blue, clear sky. One minute we were laughing and joking, the next minute bombs were falling on us.' The Americans used a total of 90 planes – 45 descended from one direction and 45 from the other. The British POWs were effectively caught in the middle.

This 'pattern bombing' was designed to hit the IG Farben complex (just a few yards from the British camp). Inevitably, not all the bombs hit their intended target.

The POWs had around five air-raid shelters sited next to their huts. These could house five hundred prisoners. The design was very basic and the structures were buried to a shallow depth. In some respects they were similar (though larger) to the Anderson shelters being used in the UK.

A bomb hit one of the entrances as the British (together with German sentries) scrambled towards the shelter. The POWs died alongside the guards. Afterwards, the prisoners dug the bodies out of the rubble and the Germans took them away. The survivors were terrified of another air raid. Doug recalls that the feelings of shock and disbelief remained in the camp for many days. Men would start to shake 'like rabbits' every time the air-raid sirens went off. They wondered if they would be killed next. The feeling was made worse as an Allied bombing run had resulted in Allied casualties.

No further British deaths occurred in the increasingly regular air raids. It was becoming clear to the POWs that the Nazis' strength was being weakened as bombers met little resistance during their sorties.

If the bombs fell when the POWs were working inside IG Farben then some of them would run into nearby fields to seek sanctuary in ditches. Others, including Brian, would remain at work to try to find a safe area in the factory. 'There was a big concrete tube which was lying horizontal on the ground,' he recounts. 'We did not know what it was going to be used for but we would sit in there when the bombs fell. On one occasion, the tube was lifted off the ground by the force of a bomb blast and there were around 15 of us in there at the time – mostly POWs. No one was hurt.'

More than 60 years later and Doug still asks why the nearby gas chambers were not targeted. By 1944, the chambers were claiming thousands of lives every day and the destruction of one of them may have slowed the pace of the Holocaust.

Brian escaped the August 1944 American bombing raid as he was suffering from paratyphoid and had been taken into the POWs' 'sick ward' (a separate hut consisting of a couple of rooms with three or four beds in each one). Despite its proximity to the blasts, it remained untouched by the commotion outside. 'I remember the explosion,' recalls Brian. 'I remember the bombs going off, it was so close. It was only 50 yards away from where I was lying. I must have been worried. It didn't last for long, about five minutes and it was all over.'

Despite his illness, Brian was asked to leave his sickbed and help with the injured. 'Other people were also helping the wounded and bringing them in. We opened up Red Cross parcels to make drinks for them whilst they were in bed. The only one (casualty) I remember had his scalp hanging off and it was hanging down by his ear – he was the most senior NCO in the camp at the time. There must have been about a dozen that were wounded and needed to lie down.'

The sick ward was very basic and primitive. A few of the POWs had trained as either medics or doctors. They were expected to run this meagre facility with little or no medicine and few supplies. Brian was cared for by an English doctor who had been in the South African Army. Captain W. O. Harrison would check on Brian's progress every morning.

Brian was only there for a week or so and he shared a room with two other men. One of them had 'gone round the twist and had a screw lose'. His mental condition was so bad that he would literally try to climb the walls to escape out of the window. Brian cannot remember if the sick bay was well stocked with medical supplies or not. Judging from official documents, the ward had minimal tablets and medical facilities and the doctors struggled to help their patients. He does recall how most of the men who went to the sick bay were ill with flu (or similar ailments) but remembers little else of his experience (except that he constantly sweated). The doctor believed he had become sick by drinking from the camp's water supply.

After the war, two of the physicians who treated the British patients (but not Brian) gave evidence to the Nuremburg war tribunals. Robert Robertson was a Scottish born Army lieutenant who had arrived at Auschwitz in September 1943. He worked alongside Dr Ian Spencer who was the physician in charge of the British POWs. Robertson recalled how they were 'told from the outset by the officials of IG Farben as well as the Farben doctors that we were expected to keep the sick list down to 3%'.[20] Depending on the accuracy of the known figures for British POWs in E715 Auschwitz, this may have meant that as little as 18 to 36 men were effectively allowed to be sick or injured at any one time. With so many men working in poor conditions, living in such cramped quarters and with such a low calorific intake, it was not surprising that the sick list soared well above the Nazi threshold.

Robertson recalled how the Germans would inspect the sick bay themselves and after a 'casual' examination 'would rule that so many men who were designated by us as unfit for work were in fact fit for work'.[21] The following morning, armed guards would march the sick men out of the hospital and straight back to the factory.

Due to his position as one of the camp's doctors, Robertson was able to move around 'reasonably freely' which allowed him to closely observe the state of concentration camp inmates. In his affidavit, he termed them as 'working corpses' and remembered how 'they were handled just the same as a herd of cattle except that one wouldn't ordinarily hold fixed bayonets and use the butt end of a rifle on the cattle'.[22]

Dr Spencer spent little time away from the ward and was horrified at the cavalier attitude the Nazis adopted towards his patients. He knew the three per cent limit was impossible to maintain and records that the actual sick rate was 'often 10% to 15%'.[23]

Based on estimations made by POWs and Jews in their post-war affidavits, this would mean 60 to 120 men (at any one time) should have been left in his care as they were unable to work. He recalled the weekly inspections by one of the German doctors who would spend a mere half a minute with each patient – before declaring them entirely fit. He also grimly remembered that the guards with 'fixed bayonets' would take the sick and injured back to the factory.

Frederick Davison ended up in the hospital with influenza. After the war, he spoke about how the Germans came into the ward and removed the patients from their beds – without even allowing them to 'put any shoes on'. Davison recounted how he quickly dressed himself and thought that the POWs would 'be in the square just a few minutes and return to the hospital'.[24] Instead they were marched to work. The POWs would normally take sandwiches (as part of their rations) for their lunch at the factory. On this particular day, the patients received an additional punishment for being sick as they found themselves with no food for the entirety of their shift.

The war was entering its closing salvos and the British would soon leave E715 Auschwitz for their long march to freedom. Doctor W. O. Harrison had nursed Brian back to health once and he was about to become Brian's saviour for a second time.

4

The Long Walk to Freedom and Recovery

By the start of 1945, it was clear that the Germans had a matter of weeks before their '1000-year Reich' was to come to an end. Their horrendous crimes would result in the Nuremburg tribunals where Nazi war criminals would face justice.

Walter Duerrfeld is a little known wartime figure. He was a senior official at IG Farben and his use of slave labour led to his trial in 1947. He stood accused of crimes against humanity alongside other members of the same company. Former British POWs testified against them. At the end of the hearing, Duerrfeld was sentenced to eight years in prison.

He kept a diary documenting the end of the war. These notes were entered as evidence at his trial and the ten-page document provides an in-depth insight into Nazi thinking during the Soviet advance. He noted that, by the summer of 1944, preparations were already being made 'for a possible evacuation order'.[1] By the start of 1945, the Nazis had detailed plans on how to destroy the factory and quickly move their staff to safety.

In the middle of January 1945, Duerrfeld noted how the

'atmosphere in the plant became more serious'. By then, the Soviets were a mere 40 kilometres away and 'Russian reconnaissance planes were constantly in the air above the plant'.

Despite the 'alarming news' from the front, the Nazis continued to try to carry out repair work on bomb damage sustained in the IG Farben factory. On Tuesday 16 January 1945, Duerrfeld wrote about the first aerial attack at night and says the experience was 'very unpleasant'. During the Wednesday morning, IG Farben's managers ordered their staff to prepare their families for a rapid departure. Duerrfeld recalled that it was a bitterly cold night when the 'evacuation trains' finally left Auschwitz.[2]

'Haversack rations' were supplied for the families to help ease the discomfort of the long journey ahead of them. By then, many of the civilian employees were refusing to work and looting was becoming a major concern. The police were called to try to protect tools and the factory. The Nazis showed greater concern for their equipment than they did for the Jews.

Slave labourers were increasingly being kept in their camps during the mornings. The lack of a workforce, however, cost the Nazis money and so they tended to force these people into work during the latter part of the day.

There was little 'food' for the workers in IG Farben as the cooks were no longer being employed and the camp was besieged by the Russians. There were also growing fears that the water supply would stop. Despite this lack of basic facilities, the Nazis were determined to keep the British soldiers working for as long as possible.[3]

The SS became more and more agitated as the situation continued to deteriorate. They were expecting their own marching orders and were, therefore, increasingly reluctant to release the Jews from their huts to go to work.

With the Soviets closing in on the camp, it was decided that the Jews would be forced to walk back to Germany. On Friday, 19 January 1945, IG Farben's slave labourers began their long march to liberation. Freedom was now within their grasp, yet many of them would die from the atrocious physical conditions they were about to endure. Their bodies would remain scattered along the same roadsides which would later be used by the British POWs. Some 850 IG Farben workers were classed as being too unfit for the journey and were left unguarded in the camp.

The Soviet's air force bombed the IG Farben complex overnight on Saturday, 20 January. They dropped incendiary devices which destroyed the British camp. During the raid, Brian ran out of the hut and sought shelter in a nearby building. On Sunday, Duerrfeld made a note in his diary that he had ordered the British POWs to leave. By then, the Soviets were a mere ten kilometres, and six days, from liberating Auschwitz.

The British were told that it simply was not safe for them to remain behind and put themselves at the mercy of the

Russians. Tensions were beginning to manifest themselves between the capitalist west and their communist ally. The birth pangs of the Cold War were being felt. The Russian Army had a brutal reputation for violence and rape – an act which they would repeatedly carry out on their arrival in Berlin. Knowing how their adversary would deal with civilians on their arrival at Auschwitz, the managers at IG Farben decided to evacuate female staff by train.[4] They left at the same time as the British, who faced several months walking through a war zone in the unrelenting cold.

'All they said was that the Russians will be here shortly and we could hear the guns firing. We were told that they would ill-treat us,' remembers Brian. 'We didn't know how far we were going, nor did we have many belongings. The camp had burnt down the night before and we were concerned that we could move at all. We only had the clothes we were standing in and a few personal items. We didn't know how long and arduous the walk was going to be.'

'We were hoping we would be released to go home and at that stage we didn't realize what was happening,' recounts Doug. 'We didn't know we were going. We were woken up and we were out – that was it. We collected clothing but after a few days they got heavy and we dumped them.'

One post-war account states that some 560 British men left E715 Auschwitz on 21 January 1945.[5] They had little food and they were about to be exposed to temperatures in excess of minus 25 degrees.[6] They would be accompanied by Ger-

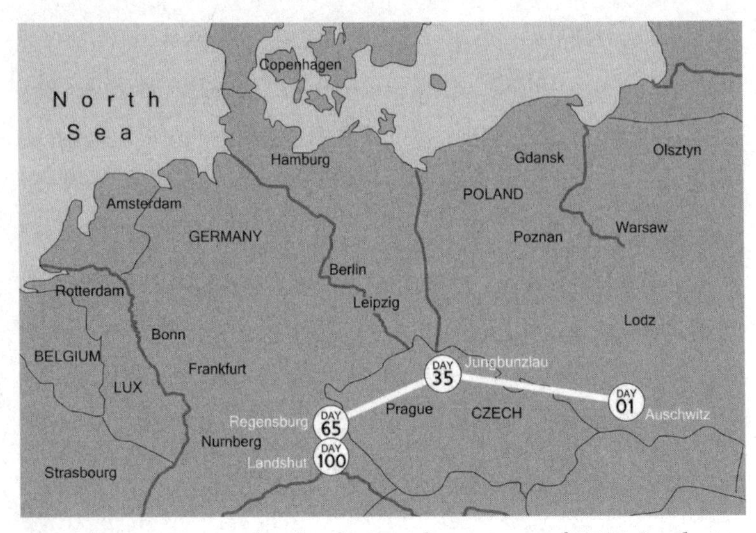

Map showing route taken by the British survivors of E715 Auschwitz, January to April 1945

man guards and POWs from other camps. Some of the men managed to note towns and villages which they passed through. By their account, the POWs covered a minimum of 526 miles during their four-month trek. Doug Bond, however, estimates that they walked many more miles than that.

'It's hard to see how it wasn't closer to 1000 miles when you think we were in Poland and we went through Czechoslovakia and continued until we got to Bavaria and the German border. We finished at Landshut which is just north of Munich.

'I think we would cover 10 to 15 kilometres a day. We would start off in the morning as a quiet bunch. By the end of the day we were stretched over a distance of half a mile. We were walking along but we didn't know what was happening. We just hoped to get home.'

Brian remembers being at the back of the column was advantageous as the soldiers in front would compact the fresh snow – making it easier for the men further behind to walk on. He says urinating in such intense cold was a major issue for the POWs. They also had to carry their own personal items which became tiring. In contrast, the German guards were able to use a horse and cart to carry their belongings. Weather and military traffic would sometimes mean the group was unable to move, which provided a much needed day (or two) of rest for the exhausted men.

He recalls the first week of their journey: 'We followed the same route as the Jews so there were dead bodies everywhere. You would walk for an hour and see one. An hour later and you might see half a dozen together by the side of the road. I estimate we saw 60 dead during the first few days. We couldn't do anything for them. We just saw them lying there and walked on.'

John Adkin recorded his POW experiences in 1947 for the war crimes tribunal. He had clear memories of the march: 'Concentration camp inmates had been evacuated from Auschwitz a few days before us in the winter of 1945. It was very cold and the inmates were thinly clad. While on the march, we frequently saw frozen inmates. We could see their arms and legs sticking out of the snow which was quite deep.'[7]

At IG Farben, the situation was rapidly worsening for the Nazis. Within three days of the British leaving, the Germans were frantically clearing the area around the factory of 'all rolling stock, including a freight car loaded with operationally vital parts and secret files'.[8]

They were running out of fuel and water. Duerrfeld noted that the factory's remaining vehicles had been requisitioned to fight the Soviets. His diary ends on Wednesday 24 January 1945 where he stated that the power plant was still operating and would remain so 'through to the end'. For them, the end would come three days later with the arrival of Stalin's army.

By then, the British POWs had managed to walk the first 69 miles of their march to freedom and had stopped to rest at a place called Kreuzendorf. Doug Bond remembers: 'Everybody was hungry and we had no food. It was an old coal mine and there were bunks where POWs, who worked in the mine, used to sleep.'

For Doug and his compatriots, it was a troubling time. 'We didn't know where we were going and were thousands of miles away from home. We were always very hungry and we never got fed so we were always looking for food. We lived on raw swede and potatoes when we could get hold of them.'

The post-war affidavits record how little food was available for the men. One man wrote, 'We were forced to march … with a ration of a two kilo loaf between 17 men for one week. Water was not available and sleeping conditions in barns were appalling … other day's rations varied such as one potato per man.'[9]

'You just kept going and hoped for the best,' says Arthur

Gifford-England. 'The guards were in the same position as us as there was nothing to eat and they scrounged like us. The general feeling was we were trying to get the hell out of it. We didn't know where we were as a start point and where we were going to go. We were going as fast as we could and just hoping to get home at some point.'

Brian remembers the constant hunger. The POWs would regularly stop at farms whereupon all the chickens would quickly disappear to feed the men. He recalls how one POW mashed potato for the group. He then deliberately used both his hands to dish out the food (so that his fingers could experience some warmth). At one point, they stumbled across sugar beet which Brian ate – resulting in colic.

'We had stopped at a sugar beet factory,' explains Brian. 'We made a stew using potatoes and sugar beet. I was in charge of one of the pots and there was a lot left over at the bottom – so I ate it. The following day we continued on the march and I had awful stomach pains. I ended up curled up in a ball by the side of the road and the column carried on.'

It was the doctor who had nursed him back to health at E715 Auschwitz who came to the young man's aid. Brian was picked up and tied to the back of the German's horse and cart. It meant that he was forced to keep walking so the effects of the colic would gradually disappear.

Cold, combined with the daily struggle to survive, eventually meant the horse became too weak to pull the cart. The men decided to kill it. Brian remembers it was a 'poor old thing that could hardly stand up'. A number of the POWs had been butchers prior to the war and soon removed the animal's vital organs. The men who had carved it up subsequently ate the heart and liver. Brian remembers the horse was served as a soup. It contained a piece of gristle which he chewed in his mouth for hours.

The forced march made its way through countries that had been under the Third Reich's control. Main roads were avoided as the immense amount of military traffic made it impractical for the POWs (and their guards) to navigate a safe passage. Consequently, they were obliged to march through woods and villages where the snow was thicker and deeper. Some of the snow was a foot deep when they started their march in January but, as the weather began to warm, so conditions became easier for the POWs. On some days, military movements would mean that they would only be able to move eight kilometres (five miles).

The improvement in the weather was of short relief to the British soldiers who soon found their footwear became one of their biggest problems. 'The soles would get so thin,' says Brian, 'that the nails would go through the soles and would sink quite deeply into your feet. When you put the boots on, you would have to slide your feet carefully back in so the nails would go back into the holes again.'

Brian, like many other men, developed frostbite during the march. One man was so badly affected that part of his foot fell off as he was easing his foot out of his boots. Brian thinks the

POW was taken to a hospital, but he never saw him again and is unsure of his fate.

At one point, one of the Germans picked up a handful of snow and smashed it into Brian's face. Another POW saw what happened and explained the guard could see the young corporal's nose had turned white. The snowball was merely a way to encourage him to rub his face to try to improve circulation before the frostbite set in.

Not all the German soldiers were quite so good-natured on the march. Several incidences of abuse against the British soldiers were reported to the United Nations War Crimes Commission. Geoffrey Amery of the Rifle Brigade who was sent to E715 Auschwitz in April 1944 estimated there were 400 men on his march. His statement recalled one occasion when they were all marched into a field during a blizzard, and were kept standing for half an hour. A different account (of the same incident) by another soldier stated the British were left for two hours in the freezing cold. This second version explained they were left outside so the German officer in charge (Meizer) could dine in a nearby house. Both affidavits, however, agree that the men suffered severe frostbite.

Amery estimated six men had to have fingers and toes amputated as a direct result of their treatment on this single occasion. He recalled one victim was a 'Private Fraser who belonged to a Scottish Regiment'. The other account stated there were more than '100 cases of frostbite, many of them serious. Captain Harrison ... saved many hands and feet by his constant attention.'[10]

On a separate occasion, a number of prisoners managed to escape from the march. Two separate post-war accounts record the Germans' response. Amery stated, 'by way of reprisal Meizer made the members of E715 spend the whole day from seven o'clock in the morning till seven o'clock at night in a field in intense cold without food. This caused great suffering.'[11] Andrew Porteous remembered protesting at their treatment alongside Captain Harrison (the medical officer). Their complaints were ignored and Porteous noted they were 'billeted into fields for eight or nine hours as a punishment'.[12]

Porteous recorded an additional incident which happened during the march and which he subsequently reported to the authorities on 1 November 1945. It related to a German called Heinz. The Second Scots Guardsman remembered the man had been nicknamed 'The Beetle' and 'The Slug' by the British.

At one point during the march he saw Heinz 'lift the butt of his rifle and strike two men on the back. I told him to stop assaulting them. He ignored me and as he was about to strike one of them again I grasped his rifle. He pushed me away. I saw him load his rifle. He pointed it at me and I threw myself to the ground as he fired. He missed me.'

Another guard intervened and stopped Heinz from continuing his assault. Porteous wrote that he was convinced that the guard intended to fire at him and he stated that the

German would repeatedly threaten 'to shoot any prisoner whom he considered was troublesome'.[13]

Neither Brian Bishop nor Doug Bond recalls any brutality on their march. Brian says the guards suffered as much as the POWs and that these incidents may have happened to a different group on one of the many routes from Poland to Germany. Doug adds that they may have been 'shoved into barns at night' but that the guards who walked alongside them were 'all the old blokes who were in the First World War and they didn't want to march anyway'.

Six men (including Arthur Gifford-England) succumbed to pneumonia within five weeks of leaving Auschwitz and suddenly found themselves abandoned in an old museum where they were nursed by two naval dentists. They were 'pulled out of the walk' so quickly that there was no chance to say goodbye to the other men. After three weeks, the six men were taken by train to Pilsen (Germany) where they joined another march.

Arthur and his five compatriots from E715 were liberated at the start of May. He remembers the huge sense of joy and relief on returning home. 'After you've been shut up for a long time with a 50 per cent chance of being killed and you see the white cliffs of Dover, there was not a dry eye on the plane.'

Sixty-eight years later and Arthur still cannot describe the extent of the horrors he witnessed in Poland. 'Looking back at E715 Auschwitz, I can't tell you the feelings that I have. To me, it was incredible that people of the same race [the Jewish

Capos] could treat their own fellow people in the way they did. When you see Jews killing Jews, you wonder what is happening. That was the worst part of imprisonment for me. The biggest problem for us was that we didn't have much to eat and we just managed to get by.' On his return, Arthur soon learnt to stay quiet about his experiences at E715 Auschwitz. 'We shut up. People don't realize we were in E715, they didn't and they don't. I just thank God we got out of it.'

After two months of walking, together with a short train journey in an open truck, the other POWs finally reached Regensburg. It was 26 March 1945 and the war in Europe would shortly come to an end. They were billeted to a small number of farm buildings located a mile away from the city. They remained at this location for a month. The city sits on the River Danube in Bavaria and had suffered bomb damage following air raids on its aircraft factory. It was a welcome break for the soldiers and morale improved, even though the Germans made them clear rubble from the streets.

'The mood was good and we were finally stationary after weeks of marching,' remembers Brian. 'We had water so we could have a decent wash as we hadn't had one for weeks. There was a general sense of relief that the march had stopped for a while.'

The crops and livestock quickly disappeared from the farm where the men were stationed as they feasted themselves on this plentiful supply of food. On one occasion, the POWs stumbled on a secret cache of potatoes which they were quick to steal. The Nazis would have needed such food for the continuing war effort. Brian remembers the farmer was unable to complain as he was illegally hiding the vegetables for himself.

By now, it was obvious to the soldiers that the war was over. It was a realization which provided comfort. The final leg of their march started on 23 April and lasted three days. The guards eventually 'disappeared' on 28 April and Brian remembers waking up to discover they had gone overnight.

The SS were fighting Allied forces nearby and the POWs had effectively been 'left to their own devices'. Some of them decided not to 'wait around' and simply walked away. It is not known if they arrived safely back in Britain.

An Allied fighter plane flew over the POWs and identified them as part of a friendly force. Doug remembers how it waved its wings at them before flying away. The pilot radioed their position to a nearby American unit who subsequently liberated the men of E715.

It was 6.30 a.m. when they saw the small American tank coming towards them. The British did not cheer but were pleased to see a friendly Allied force. After years of hardships, the POWs asked the 'Yanks' for sweets which they happily handed out to the young men. In his post war affidavit, Andrew Porteous (Second Scots Guardsman) remembered the men of E715 were liberated by a 'Captain Robertson'.[14]

Rumours quickly spread that some of the German guards

from their march had been captured and were being treated as POWs – an irony not lost on the British soldiers.

The men were desperate to return home. For the next four days, however, they were unable to move as the weather conditions steadily worsened. They became isolated on a farm which was approximately ten miles from Landshut in Bavaria. Local people opened their doors to the POWs to try to provide some comfort for the soldiers.

After they were deloused, they were transported by trucks to Landshut aerodrome where a Dakota plane, the 'Round Robin', flew them to France. They arrived in Rheims on 11 May 1945, where they stayed in an American camp before finally being flown home.

The war may have ended but, for many of these soldiers, the most arduous part of their journey was about to begin. The mental trauma of witnessing the horrors of Auschwitz would take its toll on many of the men.

Brian arrived back in Aylesbury on 15 May 1945. The experience had left its mark on the young corporal. He soon found it was difficult to cope and was medically discharged from the Army. For the next two years, Brian would regularly see a psychiatrist on a Friday afternoon at the West Hammersmith Hospital in London.

'Twelve of us would sit on long wooden benches waiting to see the psychiatrist who would sometimes turn up several hours late before the first of us went in. I was very bad tempered at the time and by the time I went to see him I was really angry. You could never smoke in there. They call it Post-Traumatic Stress Disorder nowadays. I used to have some very violent dreams.'

During his imprisonment, Brian had befriended a Jew who told him about the Nazi soldiers who had stormed into his family home. The story would become the basis of Brian's worst nightmare, a dream which he can still recount today.

He remembers the inmate's description of what happened. 'He told me how they came into his home and how one of the children wouldn't stop crying so one of the soldiers killed the child, he was only a baby, by picking him up, by his feet, and bashing his head against the wall. That was the worst dream I had. It lasted for years afterwards. There were other bad dreams as well – but I can't remember them now.'

Brian was given a medical allowance to encourage him to see the psychiatrist. Despite the financial benefits, he decided to stop the meetings, as he simply felt there was little benefit to him. His nightmares continued and it was only in the mid-1950s that his mental state began to improve.

He 'didn't realize' that he was ill and recalls how his wife became 'scared stiff' of him. 'She never knew what sort of mood I would be in. On some days nothing was right and I remember I used to want to swear at my children for simply tapping their fingers.'

Brian went on to work as a radio and television technician for various companies over a 40-year period before finally retiring in 1985. Despite his career and family life, the memories of being imprisoned in E715 Auschwitz continued to haunt him and he remained unable to talk about them.

In 2006, he wrote a short letter to the *Daily Mail* which answered a question concerning Charlie Coward's role during the war. I happened to read the letter and contacted Brian who agreed to be interviewed for this book. It was the first time that he had ever spoken about his time in Auschwitz.

'I wouldn't have opened up if I hadn't written that letter to the *Daily Mail*. I didn't even tell my wife. She knew I had been there but I never told her the details of what happened at E715. After the war, people were only interested in heroes. If you escaped from a prison camp then you became a hero. If you didn't escape then you became forgotten. In Auschwitz, it was practically impossible to escape as every bush had a soldier hiding behind it.'

Brian decided to stay quiet about his wartime experiences when he returned to life as a civilian. 'You got fed up with people bragging about what they did in the Army and I didn't really feel that my experiences mattered that much. All we were interested in was surviving. Everyone else wrote their stories about what a smashing time they had. I didn't. I wish I could have stayed in the Army though.'

In 2007, BBC South West's *Inside Out* team took Brian back to Auschwitz for the first time since he started his long march to freedom.

'I was disappointed,' recalls Brian. 'There was nothing there that I recognized, except for the old factory site, which we weren't allowed into. There was no sign of my camp or the Jewish camp.' He was told that much of it had been 'pulled down years ago'.

'We also visited the site of the main crematorium. When I was at the camp, we all knew about it but obviously we never saw it when we were there. I also saw the conditions the Jews lived in. They slept on three separate shelves that stretched from one end of their hut to the other. There must have been hundreds in there. As a POW, we only had 80 to a hut.'

On returning home, Arthur Gifford-England also found his wartime recollections difficult to discuss. 'I didn't talk about it for a long time,' he says, 'no one believed that we were at Auschwitz and no one believed what we had seen.' He also suffered from the effects of being imprisoned in E715. On one occasion he hid under his bed as a plane flew over his house. The noise reminded him of the Allied air raids which had killed so many fellow prisoners.

Doug wishes he could have told his story sooner. He says the survivors simply tried to get on with their lives once they had returned to England. In 2008, he asked, 'Would anyone have thought about writing it as a story? I don't suppose anyone would give it a second thought.'

5

The Official Record

Hundreds of post-war statements, made by British servicemen incarcerated at E715 Auschwitz, recount the daily horrors of their imprisonment. Some men could never speak of the suffering they saw in the camp. Official papers surrounding E715 Auschwitz may help to explain why so many of these returning soldiers found it difficult to adjust to normal everyday life in Britain.

There are many documents detailing German brutality in 'standard' Nazi POW camps. Life for a British prisoner at E715 Auschwitz, however, was made infinitely worse by their location. Most Allied prisoners who were housed in German camps did not watch an endless parade of brutality and death. They did, however, in E715 Auschwitz. The papers also recall their incessant hunger and how, without Red Cross parcels, they would have starved.

The affidavits included in this chapter were collated by war crime investigators. Some of these statements were made as late as 1947. It could be argued that two years is a considerable length of time between witnessing an event and recording it. An observer may assert that memories can 'alter' over a period of time as the individual's mind adjusts to the harrowing events it has witnessed. It should also be noted that the personal testimonies in this book were collected more than 60 years after liberation. With such a gulf of time between the past and present, the documents may provide a closer (and clearer) insight into life at E715 Auschwitz. Overall, much of the survivors' testimonies of 2008 accurately reflect the content of the post-war affidavits.

The overwhelming feeling from the witness statements is that the British were desperate to tell the world of the atrocities which they witnessed. Many of them had logged key events in their camp so they could pass the information to post-war investigators. They realized the Allies were moving closer to Auschwitz and felt they had a duty to try to ensure the world remembered the scale of the Nazi atrocities.

All the documents share the same theme: everyone in the camps knew of the gas chambers and that the Jews lived under the constant shadow of death.

In his affidavit, Leonard Dales recalled how one Jew realized he was going to die and made the British POW promise that he would live so he could tell the outside world about the cold, calculated manner of the death camp.[1] He explained to the shocked POW how Jewish victims were given the impression that they were going to have showers.

Dales recalled the inmate's words to him: 'Many times when they realized what was happening, terrible scenes would take place, but they were nevertheless forced into the gas chambers at pistol point by the SS.'[2]

The British POW remembers one incident in IG Farben when 'one of our boys' tossed a cigarette to a Jew 'who was loading some pipes'. He seriously cut his leg in the 'scramble' to retrieve the gift. What would normally be a fully treatable cut became an instant death sentence. The Jew turned to the British POW and said: 'I guess this is the end. It means the gas chamber for me.'[3]

The scale of slave labour at IG Farben was immense. George Longden recorded the condition of the inmates as 'skeleton-like' with 'pale yellow, deadlike' skin. His affidavit stated that, 'even if a person just visited the factory, he couldn't help notice these things since there were over 25,000 inmates who were all over the place'.[4] SS brutality among the thousands of slave labourers was commonplace.

Sick or injured concentration camp inmates seriously affected the intricate economic arrangement between the SS in Berlin and IG Farben in Auschwitz. The company paid a monthly fee of four Reichmarks for a skilled labourer. An unskilled worker cost one RM less. A sick inmate meant no productivity – and therefore lost revenue. Killing people became a matter of economics and so murder was sanctioned as a simple business decision. The SS held regular selections for gassings to ensure maximum efficiency at work. Essentially, the British were forced to watch the Jews being worked to death.[5]

By February 1944 the British had been moved to Camp Number Six. It was sited next to IG Farben but, crucially, it was within 300 yards of the concentration camp.[6] Not only did the British witness suffering in the factory but their new camp's proximity to the Jewish complex meant they were constantly aware of endless beatings and death. After the war, Frederick Davison wrote the 'inmates would be murdered in the streets in the factory grounds. I have seen the bodies themselves hundreds of times.'[7] It also meant the British would watch Jewish inmates coming to and from work – 'they weren't really walking, they just shuffled along'.[8]

In his testimony, Robert Ferris remembered a man who broke his wrist. The inmate's 15-year-old son was in tears 'not because his father's wrist was broken but because he knew that they would never bother to cure him but would send him instead to the gas chambers.'[9] He wrote about the treatment of slave labourers, 'I often saw inmates collapse in the plant and fall down dead. They were just put in the wheelbarrow and taken out of the factory.'[10]

Albert Seal returned to Edmonton in London after the war. During an average working day in the factory, he estimated that ten concentration camp inmates would collapse from exhaustion. He said these people would sometimes be picked up 'and other times they would just leave them lying in the corner. We would never see them again'. He remembers how he watched two people collapse: 'no one even tried to help them. In a short while they were both dead. The civilians working for Farben stood around laughing'. Seal estimated that the lack of food meant concentration camp inmates would not live beyond four months.[11]

Charles Hill was 22 when he was captured in 1941. In his post-war affidavit, he recounted seeing one to two people collapse every day, 'especially during the winter months'.[12] He provided his testimony to the war crimes tribunal in 1947 from his native city of Manchester. In the document, he explained how one inmate fell to his death from the top of the factory. On seeing the body, one of the Germans said, 'It is only a Jew.' The body was left for several hours.

He wrote that if an inmate was 'off for more than a certain number of days and was considered unfit for work, he would be gassed'.[13] Robert Ferris recalled inmates were admitted to a 'ramshackle hospital' where there was no medicine or bandages. He wrote, 'instead of being cured he [the patient] was done away with'.[14]

It is perhaps not surprising that the British witnessed so many inmates collapsing from exhaustion every day. Dales estimated the British would arrive to work at around 6.30 every morning and that the Jews would already be hard at work. He recalled their general appearance as 'shocking' with a 'haggard, drawn, weak (look) with pale faces and scrawny arms and legs'.[15]

Frederick Davison was 21 when he was captured at Tobruk and arrived at E715 Auschwitz in 1943. His affidavit recounted how the British termed the Jews as 'stripees' because of the 'striped pyjamas they used to wear' and how the material resembled 'sacking'. He would witness five inmates a day dying from the cold during the winter. He estimated that a reasonably healthy person, arriving in October, would be dead by the end of the year.[16]

On one occasion, Robert Ferris (together with the civilian workers) watched as the SS carried 30 dead inmates through IG Farben's main entrance and down 'into the cellar of the administration building'.[17] He attributed their deaths to 'exhaustion'.[18]

Not all the British soldiers at Auschwitz were classed as prisoners of war. Some became sentenced to live as concentration camp inmates themselves. Kenneth Lovell, from London, survived his experience as a slave labourer for the Nazis. He had been taken prisoner on 23 November 1944.

The corporal, from the Durham Light Infantry, had been imprisoned at Stalag 383 in Bavaria but had escaped.[19] Having been recaptured, he was sent to Auschwitz, whereupon 'my head was shorn and I received a striped inmate suit with a black triangle and the letters XKGF (former prisoner of war). I was not considered a prisoner of war any more and was treated like any other concentration camp inmate.'[20]

He was tasked as a labourer in IG Farben with 19 other men who had been sentenced to death. The work involved loading trucks and wagons which he described as being 'very hard' and his post-war statement recalled the regular beatings which they all had to endure. Sometimes they were hit with 'the butt of a rifle, a wooden stick, or a piece of iron or anything else that was at hand'. He was regularly hit by SS guards and the civilian workers in the factory.[21]

Lovell clearly remembered the lack of food provided to him and the rest of his unit. His affidavit to the war crimes tribunal reads, 'Our day's ration consisted of 100 grams of bread and substitute coffee or tea for breakfast; at noon we got one potato boiled in its jacket and some liquid, supposed to be soup, which on rare occasions had a piece of meat in it. In the evening we received a small portion of margarine and some tea or coffee, but no more bread. Most of the inmates were just skin and bone.'[22]

After the war, Walter Duerrfeld, the senior manager at IG Farben, lied to the Nuremburg Trials when he stated that concentration camp inmates were provided with a daily intake of '2800 calories'.[23]

Lovell remained in Auschwitz concentration camp for 24 days before being transferred to Dachau whereupon he escaped to the village of Vilseck in Bavaria. The town surrendered to him (and a number of French prisoners) shortly before American troops arrived.

Other British soldiers who had their POW status removed (and who were re-classed as concentration camp inmates) included Private Harry Ogden. He was from Otley in Yorkshire and was part of the York and Lancaster Regiment before he was captured at Narvik in April 1940. From there, he was sent to a camp in Upper Silesia where he managed to escape and spent a year fighting alongside the Polish Resistance.

When he was recaptured by the Nazis, he was armed and wearing a Polish uniform. Ogden was sent to Auschwitz with the other Polish fighters. He told his interrogators that he was an Englishman. They said he should have had 'more sense'.

The Camp Commandant sentenced Ogden to 36 lashes. He was briefly examined before he was taken with four other men into 'the middle of the compound and put on a special wooden platform which had been erected for the floggings.'[24] A riding crop was used for the punishment. Ogden fainted after eight blows and woke to find himself in solitary confinement. The following day, the Nazis started to interrogate Ogden again. He was kicked and beaten – losing two teeth in the process. Within the week, he received two additional 'public' floggings (which were carried out in front of other inmates). He remained in solitary confinement for nearly a month where his diet consisted of bread and water. A doctor saw him once to 'squeeze out the boils [which had developed on his back] and put dry dressings on'.[25]

He only spent five to six weeks in Auschwitz before being taken to a military prison where the Nazis tried him for manslaughter and sentenced him to 14 years. Ogden's war ended when he was liberated by the Russians. He returned to Britain and settled in Halifax whereupon the United Nations War Crimes' unit investigated his case.

It is hard to establish the exact numbers of British men who simply 'disappeared' into Nazi concentration camps. The reasoning for sending these men into this penal system is also unclear. Documents are littered with anecdotal evidence of soldiers who died as slave labourers for the Third Reich. Joop Zwart was a journalist from the Netherlands before being sent to Belsen. During his transport to the camp, he befriended a British prisoner (captured in Norway) called Keith Meyer. On arrival at the camp, Meyer soon fell ill with typhus and was unable to walk. The guards shot him in front of the other inmates. In his post-war affidavit, Zwart recalled Meyer came from Penwortham, near Preston.[26]

During his brief time in Belsen, conditions for the British soldier would have been exceptionally harsh. His diet would have consisted of around 200 grams of bread a day and he would have been provided with two to three pints of watery soup. The poor diet and filthy water meant disease was rife. Zwart estimated 1200 people were suffering from typhus in January 1945 alone. For the same month, he stated 4000 people were dying every week and a total of 3000 people were sick.

Based on Zwart's testimony, Meyer would have found sanitary conditions non-existent and would have been forced to share sleeping space with at least two other people. The soldier would have been worked for 12 to 14 hours a day under the constant threat of violence. Food was so scarce that Zwart remembers incidences of cannibalism and stated that inmates would murder each other to steal food.

Other British POWs who became slave labourers included a Jewish man from the north-east of England. In his affidavit,

Charlie Coward (the British POWs' Red Cross Trustee) said the man was a ship's doctor. On discovering his religion, the Nazis had sent him to the concentration camp at Auschwitz.

On hearing there were British POWs working at IG Farben, the doctor managed to get word to Coward asking him to notify the authorities and write to his family in Sunderland.

Coward decided to try to find the doctor. He made an arrangement with one of the guards to 'let me swap clothing with one of the inmates and to march into camp with [them]'.[27] He did not succeed in his mission to find the Englishman but he did manage to enter the camp. He later recorded conditions. He said the SS counted them when they left IG Farben and also when they entered the concentration camp. The living would 'hold up the dead' so the Nazis would include them in the head count. It was a move which helped increase food rations. The slave labourers were so weak that many were simply dragged back to the huts at the end of every day.[28]

When they reached their barracks, Coward's post-war affidavit continued, these people's movement was substantially restricted. Unlike the British POWs, they were not allowed to walk around. He recalled seeing the bunk beds which had to 'accommodate two or three inmates' in each one. The beds were three tiers high. Tables were in the middle where 'they would fight to get their bit of soup'. He said he spent a single night in the camp and ate potato soup with the other inmates. In the morning, they were woken up by the

Capos, who would 'kick and beat' people who 'had not gotten up'. He also noted that those 'who could not get up were just carted away'.[29]

Questions have been raised over Coward's account as some have asked how a reasonably 'healthy' looking person (such as Coward) could be surrounded by 'skeletal' inmates and yet not be spotted by the SS.

Better treatment and Red Cross parcels meant the British soldiers were far healthier in their appearance than the inmates. As George Longdon wrote in his affidavit, '[They] looked three parts dead. They were all skin and bones ... their thighs were as thin as my arms.'[30]

It may have been possible that Coward passed himself off as a recent arrival to the camp as, 'for the most part the new ones looked pretty much the same as we did, like normal, healthy human beings. After they were there a month or so, a great change ... would take place.'[31]

Even so, questions still remain. Doug Bond asks, 'He [Coward] was the man in charge of the camp so he couldn't afford to go missing, could he? When we were on parade, he was always there as he was in charge. He was always on parade when the German officer came on parade so he could never afford to go missing really.'

Brian recalls, 'When I was in the camp, I heard that a Jew had replaced Charlie Coward for a night and that he was staying in E715. I don't know if I was true. I used to talk to Charlie Coward all the time but he never mentioned it.'

Being 'in charge' did have advantages for Charlie Coward. Arthur Gifford-England remembers that his position as the Red Cross Trustee allowed him easy access to the local town. At one point, Coward managed to persuade a photographer to visit E715 and record various stills of the British POWs' football team. He also took pictures of the prisoners during their daily routine.

As early as 1942, Churchill was made aware of the plight of the British POWs – but was powerless to help. Intelligence chiefs had intercepted a Nazi report containing details on naval movements and German atrocities. The file was deemed so sensitive that it was marked for the Prime Minister's personal attention. The front page carried the words 'Most Secret' with the date: 20 July 1942.[32]

In the document, the Nazis made a request for 80 British prisoners to be used as Capos (foremen) at Auschwitz. No other document or testimony mentions POWs being used for this purpose. It seems, however, highly unlikely that the British prisoners would have assisted the Nazis. A few men, from other prisoner of war camps, joined the 'British Free Corps' – an exceptionally small group of Englishmen who fought alongside the Germans.

No surviving members of E715 are aware of any POW either joining the BFC or taking part in any activity which helped the Nazis – indeed, quite the opposite. The prisoners hated the Nazis and were sometimes forced to complete backbreaking tasks. Charlie Coward's post-war account recorded that one British POW 'dropped dead from exhaustion while working in the IG factory'. He also wrote how 'on one occasion one of our boys was beaten by a civilian' and how the clothing supplied to the POWs was 'not really good enough for the work they were doing, particularly since this was the middle of winter'.[33]

John Adkin also recalled how the POWs were abused. He said the prisoners were treated better than any other nationality but still had to work hard 'and sometimes some of our boys were struck by a guard or a foreman'.[34]

The abuse of POWs extended far beyond the barbed wire of Auschwitz.

Flight Lieutenant Edgar Jackson of the Royal Air Force was one of 168 British and American personnel who arrived at Buchenwald concentration camp on 20 August 1944. These men were no longer POWs in the eyes of the Nazis. They had been classed as concentration camp inmates and were about to be treated accordingly.

Jackson's account to war crime investigators explained how, on arrival at Buchenwald, even the 'authorities seemed surprised to see us'. All the prisoners' clothes were quickly removed and they were then completely shaved and issued with 'a thin shirt, a pair of trousers and cap, and some also got a jacket'.[35] Initially, they were forced to sleep in the open and no blankets were provided for them. After several days, 40 sheets were 'scrounged' and the men shared them out amongst themselves. They were given no shoes or socks and soon the sharp stones cut into their feet. The Nazis would make them stand on parade for 'as long as three hours' as they counted the inmates.[36]

The British POWs were left in agony due to the lack of footwear. A large number of the contingent were ill and most were suffering with 'dysentery or diarrhoea'. They were not allowed to relieve themselves during the lengthy role calls and, for many, the pain became unbearable. Eventually the men were housed in barracks where 700 inmates were expected to live 'in accommodation which would hardly hold one hundred and fifty'.[37] The overcrowding meant no one could lie down properly. Bunks were spread over four tiers and many men were left lying on the floor. There were no mattresses and, again, a lack of blankets compounded their misery.

In his affidavit, Jackson also stated that he knew of two POWs who died and one who 'went permanently deaf'. At one point, he witnessed an SS man 'strike a British prisoner a hard, swinging blow with his fist in the face'.[38]

The United Nations' war crimes commission investigated the reports of abuse after the war. It also examined the extent of disease among British POWs and how the lack of any type of medical care exasperated the situation. Its investigation grimly noted that 'Flying Officer P.D. Hemmings RAF No. 152583 died from acute rheumatic fever' whilst an inmate in Buchenwald. His death occurred at some point towards the end of September 1944. The report went on to state how large sores and fleas were all 'extremely troublesome' and that 50 Allied prisoners had been sick with 'pneumonia and pleurisy'.[39]

Lack of food was, again, a prime concern among the British soldiers whose 'meals' were issued four times a day:

At 04:00 hrs, they were given a 'half litre of thin soup or cup of coffee'.
At 07:00 hrs they received a third of a quarter of a loaf of bread with a 'small portion of margarine'.
At 11:00 hrs they were provided with a single cup of coffee (milk and sugar was not allowed).
At 16.00 hrs they received a litre of soup (in all likelihood this would have largely consisted of water).
Every second day, they received a small portion of sausage. They were also given jam or honey once a week.[40]

In October 1944, Squadron Leader Lamason noted that many of the British and American prisoners were moved from Buchenwald to Stalag Luft III, a POW camp at Sagan. It was sited within occupied Poland but bordered on Czechoslovakia. Eleven men were left behind as they were simply too ill to be moved. Seven of these inmates were Americans and four were British. Their fate is unclear. Lamason's report also noted five British people who had been deported from the occupied Channel Islands were also incarcerated at Buchenwald.[41]

Theresienstadt concentration camp became the destination

for an estimated 200 British in November 1944. They were subjected to endless brutality and atrocious living conditions. In his post-war statement, Corporal Ilott, from Ilford in Essex, recalled how three British men were unable to work as they had fallen sick. He witnessed one of the SS guards beat the ill men with a stick whilst saying, 'Here is your medicine.'[42]

The Nazis explained to the men that they were there because they were troublesome. The POWs had escaped from standard Nazi camps and so their prisoner status was being downgraded to the level of 'political prisoner'.

Theresienstadt is not as infamous as Auschwitz or Buchenwald but it was still a place filled with fear, death and violence. Situated in Czechoslovakia, more than 100,000 Jews were sent to the camp during its existence from 1941 to 1945. Tens of thousands died with many people succumbing to disease and starvation.

Lance Corporal Albert Currie, from Middlesex, was taken to Theresienstadt near the end of the war. He had 'forfeited' his POW status because he had attempted to escape from Stalag VIIIB. His head was shaved and he found himself in a room with 250 other men. Among this number were 30 British soldiers. The remaining inmates were largely Russian. His affidavit stated the living area was severely overcrowded as it could only hold a maximum of 75 people. There were two toilets and the water was 'turned off intermittently'.[43]

Eventually the 30 British men were removed and placed into a 'tunnel-like cell' which they shared with 15 other males.

Currie estimated the room was large enough for 20 men – not 45. After the war, he wrote: 'This cell was very wet, smelt very badly and we had to sleep on concrete floors. We remained in this cell for 12 days. Our food consisted of black coffee without sugar in the morning, at noon we received about a litre of watery soup and at five in the evening we received three quarters of a litre of the same soup and 300 grams of bread.' Jews were imprisoned in the cell next to the British. They were 'fed' once a week (normally Thursdays) and were forced to crawl towards the 'litre of soup' (on their stomachs) whereupon the guards would beat them.[44]

At one point, one of the British POWs in the cell became ill with malaria and pneumonia. Currie (and the others) called for a doctor to treat their comrade. Instead of providing help, the guards used a stick to beat him.

Currie remembered, 'The result of the beating on the sick man was to make him delirious and he appeared to be in a coma.'[45] His statement does not go on to explain what became of their fallen comrade but it does say that Currie believed there were no British deaths during his imprisonment at the camp.

The soldiers were also forced to dig tank traps for three days. They protested, but to no avail. Currie explained to war crime investigators that, during this time, they witnessed two Jews being shot (for not working hard enough). He also saw one punishment whereby a Czech doctor was forced to stand for twelve hours holding a 'heavy crate' above his head. He also heard that two of the British contingent had been taken away and had been beaten by the SS – because they were Jewish. Their fate remains unclear.

In the closing days of the war, the Nazis decided to move Currie and the 177 other British inmates to a part of the Flossenburg concentration camp known as Falkenau. Shortly before their departure, the British inmates were placed into a holding cell.

Five hundred men were crammed into an area designed for 75 people. The Russians slept in two lavatories which constantly overflowed with 'large quantities of filth'. There was little water and the room was 'infested with fleas'.[46] Currie managed to escape and was liberated by the Americans. It is unclear what happened to the other British men.

In a separate testimony, another British Theresienstadt detainee recalled his arrival at the camp on 14 November 1944. He wrote that all their possessions were removed from them as soon as they arrived. An American airman tried to keep a 'religious medallion' which he wore around his neck. The Nazis found it and the man was 'severely beaten'. The British prisoner was given one blanket, a spoon and a bowl before being hit around the head 'by way of welcome'. He soon realized he was lucky. He watched newly arrived Jews having their 'sticks and crutches' broken over their heads by the SS.[47]

The POW wrote his affidavit for the attention of Lt. Colonel Corballis on 6 May 1945. The events of being a concentration camp inmate were still fresh in his mind as he recalled his imprisonment at Theresienstadt. He wrote that he shared a cell with 200 people where he was forced to stand all night.

The following day the men were allowed to keep 'a towel and one piece of soap' from their kit bag before their uniforms were removed and they were shaved. They were placed into a 'small tunnel-like cell' for three weeks.

Their rations were consistently poor. At 07:00 hrs, the men received black coffee (no sugar). At midday, they received soup (with flour to 'thicken the water'). In the evening, the men were given 300 grams of bread and ¾ litre of soup. There was no soup on Sundays. Instead they received 25 grams of bread and a spoonful of jam.

On one occasion, a SS NCO forced the starving British POWs to run around the 'yard' for an hour and a half. The temperature was freezing and one man received frostbite so badly that 'after blisters had formed, he lost his nails on both hands'.[48]

The suffering these British men endured as concentration camp inmates is unimaginable. Conditions may have been better for the men who maintained their POW status at E715 Auschwitz but they were effectively observers in a modern version of Dante's *Inferno*. They were forced to witness many atrocities, but were unable to prevent the mass murder perpetuated by the Nazis. They may have tried to ease their predicament with a few games of football, but it never made their existence easier – nor did it erase the memories of their time as POWs.

At the start of 2009, Brian was one of the few surviving members of E715 Auschwitz. He said, 'People will read this book and say that we had a good time there – with our football teams and cards and things like that. People have only recently found out that I was in a POW camp as I have never spoken about it. When they ask me about it, I tell them the truth. My camp was blinking horrible.'

Notes

The research materials for this book are available to view (by appointment) at the Wiener Library in London.

IWM = Imperial War Museum

Chapter 2

1. WO 311/158 (War Office. Source: National Archives. Squadron Leader P.J. Lamason's account).
2. WO 311/158. (War Office. Source: National Archives).
3. WO 311/158 (War Office. Source: National Archives).

Chapter 3

1. NI 11693 (Affidavit from Nuremburg Trials. Source: IWM).
2. NI 11694 (Affidavit from Nuremburg Trials. Source: IWM).
3. NI 7604 (Affidavit from Nuremburg Trials. Source: IWM).
4. NI 11701 (Affidavit from Nuremburg Trials. Source: IWM).
5. NI 11699 (Affidavit from Nuremburg Trials.Source: IWM).
6. NI 9807 (Affidavit from Nuremburg Trials. Source: IWM).
7. NI 11696 (Affidavit from Nuremburg Trials. Source: IWM).
8. NI 11696 (Affidavit from Nuremburg Trials. Source: IWM).
9. NI 11694 (Affidavit from Nuremburg Trials. Source: IWM).
10. NI 11693 (Affidavit from Nuremburg Trials. Source: IWM).
11. NI 7604 (Affidavit from Nuremburg Trials. Source: IWM).
12. NI 9807 (Affidavit from Nuremburg Trials. Source: IWM).
13. NI 11696 (Affidavit from Nuremburg Trials. Source: IWM).
14. WO 309/1063 (War Office. Source: National Archives).
15. WO 309/1063 (War Office. Source: National Archives).
16. WO 311/1111 (War Office. Source: National Archives).
17. NI 11696 (Affidavit from Nuremburg Trials. Source: IWM).
18. WO 311/121 (War Office. Source: National Archives).
19. NI 11014 (Affidavit from Nuremburg Trials. Source: IWM).
20. NI 11700 (Affidavit from Nuremburg Trials. Source: IWM).

21. NI 11700 (Affidavit from Nuremburg Trials. Source: IWM).
22. NI 11707 (Affidavit from Nuremburg Trials. Source: IWM).
23. NI 11707 (Affidavit from Nuremburg Trials. Source: IWM).
24. NI 11694 (Affidavit from Nuremburg Trials. Source: IWM).

Chapter 4

1. NI 11956 (Affidavit from Nuremburg Trials. Source: IWM).
2. NI 11956 (Affidavit from Nuremburg Trials. Source: IWM).
3. NI 11956 (Affidavit from Nuremburg Trials. Source: IWM).
4. NI 11956 (Affidavit from Nuremburg Trials. Source: IWM).
5. WO 311/1112 (War Office. Source: National Archives).
6. WO 311/1112 (War Office. Source: National Archives).
7. NI 11699 (Affidavit from Nuremburg Trials. Source: IWM).
8. NI 11956 (Affidavit from Nuremburg Trials. Source: IWM).
9. WO 311/1112 (War Office. Source: National Archives).
10. WO 311/1112 (War Office. Source: National Archives).
11. WO 311/1112 (War Office. Source: National Archives).
12. WO 311/1112 (War Office. Source: National Archives).
13. WO 311/1112 (War Office. Source: National Archives).
14. WO 311/1112 (War Office. Source: National Archives).

Chapter 5

1. NI 11695 (Affidavit from Nuremburg Trials. Source: IWM).
2. NI 11695 (Affidavit from Nuremburg Trials. Source: IWM).
3. NI 11695 (Affidavit from Nuremburg Trials. Source: IWM).
4. NI 11703 (Affidavit from Nuremburg Trials. Source: IWM).
5. NI 4184 (Affidavit from Nuremburg Trials. Source: IWM).
6. NI 11695 (Affidavit from Nuremburg Trials. Source: IWM).
7. NI 11694 (Affidavit from Nuremburg Trials. Source: IWM).
8. NI 11706 (Affidavit from Nuremburg Trials. Source: IWM).
9. NI 11693 (Affidavit from Nuremburg Trials. Source: IWM).
10. NI 11693 (Affidavit from Nuremburg Trials. Source: IWM).
11. NI 11708 (Affidavit from Nuremburg Trials. Source: IWM).
12. NI 11704 (Affidavit from Nuremburg Trials. Source: IWM).
13. NI 11704 (Affidavit from Nuremburg Trials. Source: IWM).
14. NI 11693 (Affidavit from Nuremburg Trials. Source: IWM).
15. NI 11695 (Affidavit from Nuremburg Trials. Source: IWM).
16. NI 11694 (Affidavit from Nuremburg Trials. Source: IWM).
17. NI 11693 (Affidavit from Nuremburg Trials. Source: IWM).
18. NI 11693 (Affidavit from Nuremburg Trials. Source: IWM).

19. NI 11702 (Affidavit from Nuremburg Trials. Source: IWM).
20. NI 11702 (Affidavit from Nuremburg Trials. Source: IWM).
21. NI 11702 (Affidavit from Nuremburg Trials. Source: IWM).
22. NI 11702 (Affidavit from Nuremburg Trials. Source: IWM).
23. NI 4184 (Affidavit from Nuremburg Trials. Source: IWM).
24. WO 311/149 (War Office. Source: National Archives).
25. WO 311/149 (War Office. Source: National Archives).
26. WO 309/17 (War Office. Source: National Archives).
27. NI 11696 (Affidavit from Nuremburg Trials. Source: IWM).
28. NI 11699 (Affidavit from Nuremburg Trials. Source: IWM).
29. NI 11696 (Affidavit from Nuremburg Trials. Source: IWM).
30. NI 11703 (Affidavit from Nuremburg Trials. Source: IWM).
31. NI 11698 (Affidavit from Nuremburg Trials. Source: IWM).
32. HW 1/761 (Intelligence report to PM. National Archives).
33. NI-11696 (Affidavit from Nuremburg Trials. Source: IWM).
34. NI 11699 (Affidavit from Nuremburg Trials. Source: IWM).
35. WO 311/158 (War Office. Source: National Archives).
36. WO 311/158 (War Office. Source: National Archives).
37. WO 311/158 (War Office. Source: National Archives).
38. WO 311/158 (War Office. Source: National Archives).
39. WO 311/158 (War Office. Source: National Archives).
40. WO 311/158 (War Office. Source: National Archives).
41. WO 311/158 (War Office. Source: National Archives).
42. WO 311/199 (War Office. Source: National Archives).
43. WO 311/199 (War Office. Source: National Archives).
44. WO 311/199 (War Office. Source: National Archives).
45. WO 311/199 (War Office. Source: National Archives).
46. WO 311/199 (War Office. Source: National Archives).
47. WO 311/199 (War Office. Source: National Archives).
48. WO 311/199 (War Office. Source: National Archives).

Picture credits: front cover photograph, p. 11 (top), p. 23 & p. 43, courtesy Arthur Gifford-England; frontispiece map courtesy US Holocaust Memorial Museum, Washington DC (redrawn by Usfor Design and Print Ltd, Liskeard); p. 7 (top), courtesy Brian Bishop; p. 7 (bottom), p. 9 (bottom) & p. 11 (bottom), courtesy Duncan Little; p. 9 & p. 40, courtesy Doug Bond; p. 31, public domain; p. 54, drawn by Usfor Design and Print, Liskeard.